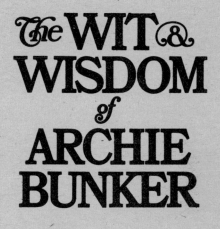

The WIT & WISDOM of ARCHIE BUNKER

ALL IN THE FAMILY

directed by John Rich

Contributing Writers:

Tom & Helen August
Bill Dana
Elias Davis
Henry Garson
Susan Harris
Paul Harrison
Bryan Joseph
Lee Kalcheim
Austin & Irma Kalish
Norman Lear
Alan J. Levitt
Jerry Mayer
Philip Mishkin
Warren Murray
Don Nicholl
Tina & Les Pine
David Pollock
Rob Reiner
Michael Ross
Stanley Ralph Ross
Sandor Stern
Burt Styler
Paul Wayne
Lennie Weinrib
Bernie West
Steve Zacharias

"Those Were The Days"
Theme song by
Lee Adams and Charles Strouse

Compiled by Eugene Boe

A Marvin Glass & Associates Presentation

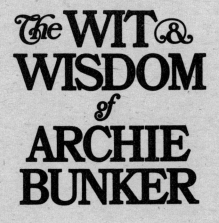

The WIT & WISDOM of ARCHIE BUNKER

POPULAR LIBRARY • NEW YORK

FOREWORD

Fourteen short months ago, as this is written, Archie Bunker was born. For an infant, he certainly has had a lot to say! And incredibly enough, a portion of it has already entered the language of our times. "Stifle!" "Dingbat." "Meathead." "You're a pip, a real pip!" Etc.

Some of Archie's longer speeches are more difficult to remember verbatim, however, and we receive countless letters wanting to know what Archie said about such-and-such on this or that show. THE WIT + WISDOM OF ARCHIE BUNKER covers most of these requests. With the image of that incomparable talent, Carroll O'Connor, firmly fixed in your mind—hear, then, the voice of Archie Bunker.

NORMAN LEAR

FROM THE MAILBAG OF ARCHIE BUNKER

Dear Archie:

The whole country's talking about you. You must know that.

Everywhere one goes these days people are quoting you on a thousand things. In fact, there do not seem to be many topics on which you have *no* opinion.

It remains to be seen whether you have the solutions to everything that ails our society. But if there is one thing America does have going for it, it is a sense of humor. And I honestly believe if there's one thing that can bring us together, it is people sharing a good laugh. With tens of millions of Americans laughing along with Archie Bunker, I have hopes we can pull together in other ways too.

I'm glad someone got the bright notion to collect some of your choicest bon mots. I predict they will enjoy even wider circulation than the quotations of Chairman Mao. God knows, they're a lot funnier!

Most sincerely,
Marvin Glass
Chicago, Illinois

CONTENTS

ARCHIE-ISMS

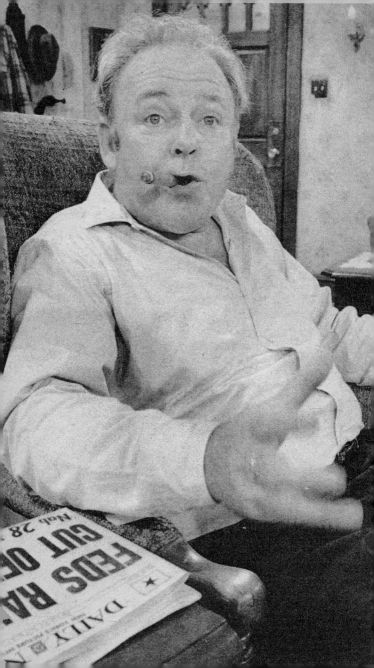

**Archie's command
of the language is legionary.**

I'm gonna have to lay down some ground rules and
  priorororities.

* * * * *

I always said those two was right outta Science Fric-
  tion.

* * * * *

I give ya the biggest build-up since Grant took Richard.

* * * * *

Well, goodbye and good ribbons.

It was said under dupress.

* * * * *

This woman could be a kidnapper making you an excessity after the fact!

* * * * *

The statements I made were supposed to be sub-rosy.

* * * * *

Don't take everything so liberally.

* * * * *

Nobody gets arrested in this country lest he deserves it! If he don't yell "pig" or none of them other epaulets, he'll be okay.

* * * * *

A woman is a frail vessel. Carried along on the ties of her emotions, she could easily flounder on the shores of tribulation.

* * * * *

Comin' in here full of ascusations . . :

* * * * *

I come home and tell you one o' the great antidotes of all times, an item of real human interest, and you sit there like you're in a comma.

* * * * *

Mr. McKinsey, you got my whole felt cooperation. Ask

me anything. Nobody takes the Fourth in this house!'

* * * * *

He's got some big move up his sleeve that he can't re-
vulge yet!

* * * * *

There's somethin' rotten in Sweden, Edith. Call it a father's intermission . . . but I smell a rat.

* * * * *

You're taking it out of contest.

* * * * *

You sound like a regular Billie Sol Graham!

* * * * *

You send kids out for a normal education and they
come back with these preversions.

* * * * *

Awright now. That's enough with the utopian tubes.
I'm eatin'.

* * * * *

Okay, okay. That's it for the anniversary. Party's over.
Let's clean this mess up. Them eggs are starting to
foment.

* * * * *

Rudy and me was as close as two peas in a pot.

5

We got a regular Edna St. Louis Millet here.

* * * * *

Straighten that picture up. He'll be here any second now and we don't want people thinkin' we live in no pig's eye.

* * * * *

"Two hundred arrested at Vietnam Day peace demonstration." If ya ask me, they oughta throw the whole bunch of 'em in jail. Look at this . . . throwin' debriss at officers of the law . . . Desecrating on the American flag.

* * * * *

What am I, a clairavoyage or somethin'? How do I know what's in there?

* * * * *

This political percussion is over as of here and now.

* * * * *

Now lay off the social menuneties.

* * * * *

'Cause you're a meathead! I been makin' my way in this world a long time, sonny boy, an' one thing I know—a man better watch out for number one! It's the survivor of the fitness!

* * * * *

What you see here is a frigment of your imagination.

Why don't you write a letter to dear Abie?

* * * * *

That's all right, Gloria. Sticks 'n stones don't break my
bones... but names'll always hurt me.

* * * * *

C'mon, Edith. Cut it out. These things ain't exactly
hairlooms, you know.

* * * * *

Forget it. It's irrevelant. It ain't German to this conversation.

* * * * *

You work? I'll believe that when hell freezes under.

* * * * *

What're you doin' with that fermometer? I'm the guy
with the temperature.

* * * * *

Don't you never read the papers about all them un-
flocked priests running around? This here priest
ain't Kosher and never was.

* * * * *

You coming here, a priest, hiding behind your hassock
—and trying to turn a dent in the fender into a pot
of gold.

* * * * *

(*About Mike*) Listen to our world traveler, will ya. Ain't never been past the Chicago Stock Yards, and now he's a regular Marco Polish.

* * * * *

He has the infrontery to imply that . . .

* * * * *

What is this, the United Nations? We gotta have a whole addenda? I'll talk to you when I get back.

* * * * *

If tampering with the United States mail is a federal offense, so is excitement to riot.

* * * * *

Cold enough to freeze a witch's mitt.

* * * * *

She's hangin' around my neck like an Albacross.

* * * * *

I don't need their whole Dun and Broadstreet.

* * * * *

Just who in hell are we entertaining here tonight? The Count of Monte Crisco?

* * * * *

Wages and prices. It's what you call your spiral staircase.

* * * * *

Whoever sent 'em obviously wanted to remain unanimous.

* * * * *

We've got the world's grossest national product.

* * * * *

(*To Gloria, about her former boyfriends*) I remember some of them beauties you hung around with, and they wasn't exactly no "Madonises."

* * * * *

He's comin' right over to shake us down. The dent in the fender ain't even cold yet, and he's comin' over to claim his pound of fish.

* * * * *

The Mets winnin' the pennant . . . . that would be a miracle. Yeah . . . like the immaculate connection.

* * * * *

You're invading the issue.

* * * * *

You and that Reverend Bleedin' Heart Felcher up there in his ivory shower.

* * * * *

No, Edith. I was out expectin' the street lights.

* * * * *

I received your leaflet at my home residence and the

words "substantial profit" fought my eye.

* * * * *

What do you mean by that insinuendo?

* * * * *

If you was half as sick as me, you'd be layin' on that floor waitin' for Rigor Morris to set in.

* * * * *

If you two malinjerers want anything . . .

* * * * *

Boiling it down to words of two syllabubs . . .

* * * * *

And who are you supposed to be—Blackberry Finn?

* * * * *

It's like looking for a needle in a hayride!

* * * * *

Looking like it's straight outta Missile Impossible . . .

* * * * *

You been standing on that phone like a pillow of salt.

* * * * *

Let's take a look here and see what new subversion you got fermentin' here.

* * * * *

10

Spare me the cleechays, Edith.

* * * * *

You've got a warfed sense of humor.

* * * * *

Watch out for that rigidness, Edith. It'll warf your personality.

* * * * *

How'd I know you had extensions to bein' an egghead.

* * * * *

You're about as funny as a crotch.

* * * * *

I call Chinese food chinks 'cause that's what it is ... chinks. There was no slurp intended against the Chinese.

* * * * *

Your mother-in-law and me don't make no fatish over birthdays.

* * * * *

I'll let you know when I—in my intimate wisdom—decides that the time has ripened.

* * * * *

The man don't have one regleaming feature.

* * * * *

11

It's just a pigment of your imagination.

*　*　*　*　*

It's like trying to make a sow's purse outta silk!

*　*　*　*　*

ARCHIE AND EDITH

The first couple of America ...
just rapping

Archie: That's you, all right. "Edith the Good!" You'll stoop to anything to be good. You'll never yell, you never swear. You never make nobody mad. You think it's easy livin' with a saint? Even when you cheat, you don't cheat to win. You cheat to lose! You ain't human!

Edith: That's a terrible thing to say, Archie Bunker. I'm just as human as you are.

Archie: Oh, yeah ... then prove you're just as human as me. Do somethin' rotten.

* * * * *

Edith: Well, Archie, I thought it would make you feel better if I let you win.

15

Archie: Let me win? That'll be the day when I can't win without you lettin' me win! I was winnin' before you let me win! You spoiled the whole thing! From here on in you wanna do somethin' together, do it together by yourself!

* * * * *

Edith: . . . Do you like being alone with me?
Archie: Certainly I like being alone with you. What's on television?

* * * * *

Edith: The other day I came across our copy of Glenn Miller's "Moonlight Serenade." You remember how we used to dance to that . . . Remember how I used to snuggle up against your cheek . . .
Archie: Oh, c'mon. Willya act your age? Even Fred Astaire and Ginger Rogers don't dance together no more.

* * * * *

Archie: Did you ever think of takin' a shot at me, Edith?
Edith: No.
Archie: That's good. And I never wanted to shoot you neither. It's nice when people get along together. Right, Edith?

* * * * *

Edith: Archie—do you realize this is the first time we been alone in years, we got eight days ahead of us. Oh my! I feel like I did on our honeymoon, all goose-pimply.
Archie: Yeah, I remember that . . . I could hardly

16

find ya behind all them bumps.

* * * * *

Archie: All right, Edith. Let's have it. I know that look. That's your family's trademark. You'se all get that look when somethin's festerin' up inside a you. Skinny around the nose and all froze up around the mouth. That's the way they was lookin' at me the day I married you. So, let's get it all out, Edith. What is it?

Edith: Well, I was just thinking. In all the years we been married you never once said you was sorry.

Archie: Edith, I'll gladly say that I'm sorry—if I ever do anything wrong.

* * * * *

Edith: And he's your cousin, Archie. How could I say no?

Archie: This way, Edith—"No." But maybe that's too much for you—it's got a whole syllable.

* * * * *

Archie: How are ya gonna play a game of rummy without beer?

Edith: I said I was sorry.

Archie: "Sorry" ain't gonna clench my thirst.

* * * * *

Edith: Your breakfast, Archie. A bacon soufflé.

Archie: Bacon soufflé! What's them weeds growin' out of the top?

Edith: That's parsley.

Archie: What happened to my eggs over easy and my

crisp bacon?

And every Sunday of my life what do you fix me for breakfast?

Edith: Prune juice—just six ounces; eggs over easy —drain the grease; crisp bacon—drain the grease; three slices of toast—not too dark; toast buttered lightly—with extra butter on the side. And coffee. Mountain grown.

Archie: Right. And I don't want no cheerful change from the humdrum fare you just enumerated. Bacon and eggs, please.

Gloria: But Daddy, bacon soufflé *is* bacon and eggs. They're all mixed up together.

Archie: I'll mix up my own bacon and eggs, if you don't mind—the way I been doin' all my life —in my stomach! Now let me have an Archie Bunker breakfast, will ya! And you can mail *this* thing to Charles de Gaulle!

Gloria: Charles de Gaulle died, Daddy.

Archie: Before he even ate it?

* * * * *

Archie: They don't take into account men's hormones. Now, I can't get into that with you, Edith. It's too male, and it's too rough. But when his hormones is acting up, I wouldn't trust any man as far as I can throw him.

Edith: But then that would include you, Archie?

Archie: Not necessarily. Because I don't let my hormones act up.

* * * * *

Edith: Listen to me, Archie—in two weeks you'll have him readin' William Berkeley.

Archie: Buckley, Edith. William Buckley.

Edith: See there? Look how fast you knew Berkeley was wrong! What *is* Berkeley anyhow?

Archie: Used to be a steak sauce. Now it's a college where they make trouble.

* * * * *

Edith: I just can't say, Archie. You don't like to hear about such things.

Archie: Edith, *what* kind of a problem are they having?

Edith: It's sexual.

Archie: Edith, you know I don't like to hear about such things!

* * * * *

Archie: We can suspense with the hellos, Edith. How come you're so late from the market?

Edith: A little boy got his braces caught in my shopping basket.

* * * * *

Archie: If you're gonna have your change of life, have it right now! You got exactly thirty seconds ...change!

Edith: Can I finish my soup first?

Archie: Forget the soup. It's lousy! Get on that phone and call up the Lodge and confirm the Bunkers is goin' to Florida as pre-deranged.

* * * * *

No, Edith, I never hated Emily. I like your Cousin Emily and them four cute teen-agers and that husband of hers is a real swell guy and ... and ... No! I don't mean a word of this. He ain't no swell

19

guy and he never was...he's a bum and she's a crank! And I hate 'em four rotten kids...And the only way you'll get me to Scranton is if some screwball hijacks the plane! I know all about your women's troubles but when I had that hernia that time, I didn't make you wear the truss!

* * * * *

Archie: You see that! After that doctor tells me to use all of that soft soap...I showed youse all how to handle the change of life. And you remember that...And now we're back to normal. You get that number, Edith?

Edith: No, you get it yourself. I don't wanna go to Disney World. I don't wanna go any place.

Archie: Back to the groinocologist!

* * * * *

Edith, was I talking too fast, or have you got slow ears? Now stifle! Your brain gets clogged. It starts backin' up on you. And there ain't no Drano for the braino!

* * * * *

Your family! Not mine! They don't know me until they want something! Seven years ago—out of the blue—Wendell's mother calls, "Hello, Uncle Archie." All of a sudden I'm elected into the family! To be the official patsy! So's I could buy Wendell's first policy. And this is his thank you note!... Canceled!

* * * * *

Edith: Hello, Archie. I'm glad you're early. Wendell

20

called and he's coming over before dinner.

Archie: I'm all for that, Edith! 'Cause if I hadda face that bum on a full stomach, I'd deterger-ate . . .

* * * * *

(Edith heaves sigh)

Archie: What was that for?

Edith: What, Archie?

Archie: What was that for?

Edith: No, I didn't mean "what?" meaning "what did you say, Archie?" I meant "what?" meaning "what was what for?"

Archie: What other "what" was there? The sigh, Edith. You heaved a sigh.

Edith: Did I sigh?

Archie: Yes, you sighed. . . And you heaved it right over here, it's like eatin' in a wind tunnel.

* * * * *

Christmas Day at The Bunkers

Edith: Maybe that's it, Archie . . . we don't have no chestnuts roasting on the fire.

Archie: Edith . . . how long have we lived in this here house?

Edith: Twenty years, Archie.

Archie: And in all them twenty years, Edith, did you ever happen to notice a fireplace around here?

Edith: No.

Archie: How are you gonna have roast chestnuts, Edith, if the house isheated by radiators?

Edith: You're right, Archie, radiated chestnuts wouldn't be the same.

* * * * *

Oh, sure, Edith. You put me into banktruptcy feedin'
'em panhandlers.

* * * * *

Why don't you answer the door? That's what I hate
about this time of year. Everyone's on the make,
even the churches.

* * * * *

Stifle, Edith. Let's have a little Silent Night around
here for a change.

* * * * *

Edith, you're scraping a nerve! When you was a kid I
think someone must have dropped you on your
throat.

* * * * *

Archie: Don't Scrooge me. I'm the only one around
here thinking of the real solemn meaning of
Christmas. Which is supposed to be a time of
peace and quiet contemplation.

Edith: But I think you're allowed to be jolly too.

Gloria: Yeah ...

Archie: Sure, Edith, I never said you shouldn't be
jolly. Just be jolly with your mouth shut ...
Just sit and think.

Edith: Think what, Archie?

Archie: Oh, don't be a dingbat. Think Religious
thoughts.

* * * * *

Archie: Sweet Tiparoos—smells like they was dipped
in a can of Flit!

22

Mike: Archie, just 'cause you're in a bad mood, you don't have to say our presents stink.

Archie: I never used that word 'stink.' All I meant was—presents should be individual.

Mike: Oh, like the present you gave us? A box of His and Hers handkerchiefs.

Archie: If you don't want 'em, give 'em back. I keep telling ya, we didn't get a Christmas bonus this year.

Edith: It's the thought that matters—I love my "Her" handkerchiefs, Archie. How did you ever get them to split a box?

*   *   *   *   *

Edith: Oh, my, red wine. I bet it's Manischevitz.

Archie: No, Edith—this is domestic.

*   *   *   *   *

How could you mix up Kaopectate with Milk of Magnesia? It's like mixin' prune juice with radiator seal.

*   *   *   *   *

Edith, all right. We both own the house, we both own the furniture and we both own the window. Half and half. And I want my half closed. Now stifle, will ya?

*   *   *   *   *

After twenty-four years of stifles, the dingbat turns on me!

*   *   *   *   *

What's so important about this time of her life? I

ain't understood no other part of your mother's life neither.

* * * * *

I gotta keep agreein' with her and being patient with her, and nice to her. I wanna tell you something . . . it's really a lousy thing, this change of life. A man's got no say in it at all.

* * * * *

Well, ain't you nervous with your mother actin' so crazy. And I don't see why you had to drag me to her doctor . . . this groinocologist guy.

* * * * *

Edith: A present for me? Oh, Archie!
Archie: All right, Edith, all right. It ain't the Pope Diamond.

* * * * *

That there is for your condition, Edith. It's for when you get one of them hot flushes.

* * * * *

Archie: I found your eyelashes, Edith. Here they are . . . in my soup.
Edith: I'm sorry, Archie.
Archie: That's okay, Edith. They wasn't in the part where I was eatin'.

* * * * *

You got that look you had when you used one of my bowling shirts to stain your spice rack. And the time

24

you gave fifty cents to the Black Panthers 'cause
you thought it was to Save Our Wildlife.

* * * * *

"Gloria and Mike have been with us one full year as
man and wife!" Yeah, that's exciting, Edith. It's like
celebrating the 365th day of a toothache.

* * * * *

Ain't the first anniversary the "paper" anniversary,
Edith? Yeah? Well, then, I'm right in the spirit! I'm
reading the paper!

* * * * *

Edith: They say if two people enjoy being alone together, that's the acid test of a good marriage.
Archie: Well, I do—okay? We got a 100 percent acid
marriage!

* * * * *

No, Edith, I didn't go out to get the paper. I heard
Macy's department store was for sale and I ran out
to put down a deposit.

* * * * *

Edith: Archie's cousin Rudy, Bertha's boy, lives out
there in El Monte. El Monte. Ain't that pretty! Just imagine, he says in the morning you
just stick your hand out the bedroom window,
and pick an orange off a tree.
Archie: You do that in New York, they mug your
hand.

I always knew what a great poetress you was from the poem you wrote me when I was sick.

"Get well quicklv.
Oh, please do.
'Cause I'm crying,
Boo-hoo-hoo."

* * * * *

The woman of the house don't collect all the milk into one bottle, that way protecting the sanity of her husband which in this house is driving him nuts!

* * * * *

Your own cousin from the hospital empties bedpans, don't make him out to be a specialist.

* * * * *

Edith, will you learn your place! You got no business in an intelligent discussion of theology.

* * * * *

Edith, let me be the doctor, huh. You got all you can handle bein' a dingbat.

* * * * *

You was with that Flenderhook character, with the bi-cuspid out to here—practically in front of his nose. Kissing him musta been like kissing a nail. Though I know you told me you never done it.

* * * * *

Playing Monopoly

Edith: I have to go to jail.
Archie: Good. Make it solitary confinement.

* * * * *

Edith: But what if it was a mistake? What if the cigars was meant for an Archie *Bink*er?
Archie: Then meet Archie *Bink*er. (*Sniffing cigar*) Edith, this is the nectarine of the Gods.

* * * * *

Edith: Come, Archie. It won't be so bad in the kitchen. Remember Arthur? He ate in the kitchen all the time.
Archie: But, Edith, Arthur was a cat.

* * * * *

Edith, the next time you want to time anything, just let the sand run outta your head!

* * * * *

How you gonna explain it to the neighbors? An extra kid shows up all of a sudden! This is the kinda thing happens to the coloreds, not to us!

* * * * *

Edith, why don't you just buy me a gun I can shoot myself with? It won't be so messy. I just cut myself four times in three seconds. Pieces of my face is down the drain on the way to the ocean. One of these days I will probably de-head myself. For the last time . . . *don't use my razor.*

* * * * *

27

I don't understand you, Edith. Your own daughter, flesh of your blood, walks out of this house every morning for the past three weeks to take off her clothes in front of a man who (a) ain't her husband and (b) makes her husband look like a pile of inner tubes. Where's all that modesty she used to have? I remember once walkin' into the bathroom accidentally after she got out of the shower—she was maybe ten years old then—and you should have heard her scream and carry on. And Edith, there wasn't even nothing to see yet!

* * * * *

Archie: That's the last of them husband and wife Lodge meetings you're draggin *me* to. Standin' around all that time talking with Freddie Wilchik. Good gravy, why are people so *boring*?

Edith: But Archie, I heard you talking to Freddie Wilchik. You talked about politics and you talked about the war and you talked about the Lodge, and you talked about down at the plant, and Freddie Wilchik hardly never said a word.

Archie: That's exactly my point, Edith. Why are people so *boring*?

* * * * *

We came back early because you went crazy in the ocean! Instead of standing next to me in the water, holdin' the ropes, your mother turns over on her back and floats out to sea like she was Moby Dick! The giant white dingbat!

* * * * *

Edith: (*with Kleenex*) Here you are, Archie.

Archie: I don't wanna paper the walls! I just want to blow my nose.

Edith: I wanted to give you a choice, Archie. There's the floral print. And here's the pioneer pattern. And these are the decorator dainties... or maybe you'd like the Great Works of Art Pattern?

Archie: Ain't you got one I can just blow my nose into without feelin' like I ruined a thing of beauty forever?... I'll take the Rembrandt.

* * * * *

Edith: I don't see what you're so upset about, Archie. I remember when you used to picket.

Archie: That was different! I was walking the picket line for my union. We didn't run screaming in the streets and blocking traffic. We did it the American way—on the sidewalk. Walking up and down dressed nice and carrying our signs. Peaceful. No violence.

Edith: Except when someone crossed the line. Then you broke his head.

Archie: That wasn't violence, Edith. That was education. It was the only way to teach those fink scabs a lesson!

* * * * *

Edith: Do you love me?

Archie: Edith, where the *hell* are you getting these questions from?

Edith: In *Fiddler on the Roof* she asks him (*singing*) "Do you love me?" I heard it before on the radio. And the man in the song, he couldn't answer her directly, either.

Archie: Well, I ain't no Fiddler on the Roof! I answer that question every day—by the fact I live with you and take care of you. I go to work and come home, go to work and come home...

ARCHIE AND MIKE

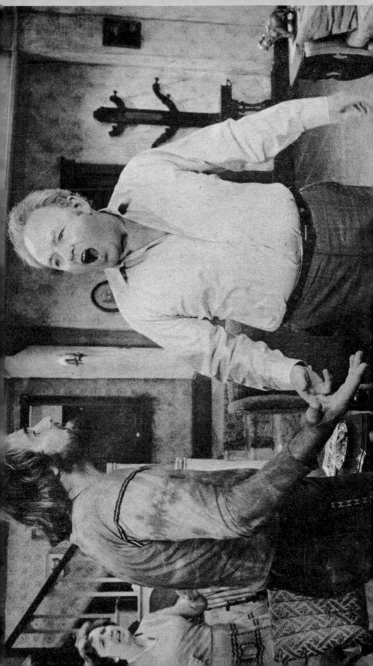

If they can just keep the
dialogue going . . .

Listen, little girl—whenever people ask me what kind
of man I want my daughter to marry, I say "I don't
care. So long as she loves him and he's white". Now,
there's a third condition. He can't be *that* guy!

* * * * *

All her life, the girl waits for "Mr. Right" and now she
settles for "Mr. Wrong/Ski"!

* * * * *

You always had a knack for pickin' losers. And I got
a feelin' with all this fuss you're making this character is gonna be the biggest loser of them all.

Edith: Mike and Gloria are gonna get married and live with us.

Archie: What am I supposed to do, join the Navy?

Edith: Archie, you know how you always prayed for a son. Well, now your prayers are answered. The Good Lord must have heard you.

Archie: In forty-seven years, he answers one prayer . . . and it had to be this!

* * * * *

Mike: Gloria, come on, hurry up! We'll miss the bus.

Archie: She missed that the day she said "I do" to you.

* * * * *

Archie: In this house it's my country right or wrong!

Mike: That's outmoded thinking, Archie. It doesn't work. And in today's society if a thing doesn't work you throw it out.

Archie: Well, you don't work. Maybe we oughtta throw you out!

* * * * *

The last time I saw him lift a hand around here was testing his deodorant.

* * * * *

There he is, Mr. Liberal Ignoramus himself.

* * * * *

It's too bad your mouth isn't connected to your brain, 'cause then maybe it would shut up.

* * * * *

Mike: I'm sorry. The wine went to my head.

Archie: I ain't surprised. There ain't nothin' else up there.

* * * * *

Archie: This house is a helluva lot better than all them fancy new houses they're building, with walls so thin you can see right through them!

Mike: So is the pyramid but who'd want to live there?

Archie: You would, if they let you in for nothin'.

* * * * *

My problem is down at work which you know nothing about. Like you said, it's a man's problem. And that lets you off the train.

* * * * *

Better not remind me of the night we met, meathead! 'Cause *that* evening is indeniably etched in my heart along with other strong memories of the past—like Pearl Harbor and the crash of the *Hindenburg*!

* * * * *

Mike: What do you mean—America: Love it or leave it?

Archie: That's right, it's a free country, so amscray.

Mike: But would our leaving solve? With or without protesters, we'd still have the same problems.

Archie: What problems?

Mike: The war. The racious problem. The economic problem. The pollution problem.

Archie: Well, if you're gonna nitpick . . .

* * * * *

You don't know much anyway. I want to tell you something. You are a person of very little quality. You have no appreciation of some of your fine things.

* * * * *

Mike: You have an untutored mind.
Archie: And I didn't go to no college to get it, either.

* * * * *

You're the one that's pollutin' my environment.

* * * * *

You're defective. No doubt about it there's somethin' broken off in there and it's ledged between the nervous system and the brain and there ain't a store in the country that would refuse to take you back.

* * * * *

Mike: You afraid I might spill the beans, Arch?
Archie: If they opened your head, that's all that *would* spill—beans.

* * * * *

Gloria: I just came by to pick up a few things.
Archie: (pointing to Mike) Well, I hope he's one of them.

* * * * *

Archie: Suppose everyone ran off to one of the communes. Who'd run the machines—who'd drive the subways? How would I get to work?
Mike: Archie, not everybody's gonna run off to a commune. It's a question of each man doing

	his own thing. Your thing is grubbing for a living in this polluted, crime-ridden city.
Archie:	And your thing is spongin' off my thing.

* * * * *

| *Archie:* | Me? Get hurt? They can't hurt *me*. I fought with Patton for three years. |
| *Mike:* | Yeah? What about? |

* * * * *

| *Mike:* | Going to college isn't easy, you know. It's hard work. |
| *Archie:* | Oh, for you, it's like building the pyramids. But anyway, studyin' sociology, preparin' to be some kind of a Do-Good Charlie ain't my idea of hard work! |

* * * * *

| *Archie:* | He wants to help the underprivileged, let him start with himself. He's got no ambition, no brains—and if that ain't underprivileged, I don't know what is. |

* * * * *

| *Edith:* | Archie, did you hear that? He said they might never come back. |
| *Archie:* | Are you kiddin'! We ain't losin' him till we sell the refrigerator. |

* * * * *

| *Archie:* | If he was on the *Titanic*, he wouldn't stop eatin' till the water came up over his nose! |

* * * * *

Mike:	It's too tough, Gloria. I've decided I'm gonna quit college and get a job.
Gloria:	Michael, don't be childish!
Archie:	No, no. Be childish, Michael! Be childish!

* * * * *

Archie: You can't move outta here. You can't go to night school and work and support a wife and kid and pay for an apartment. First of all, you ain't got the brains!

* * * * *

You remind me of Marty Prendergast. I told you about him, Edith. Skinny little kid, always wet under the nose. He was the *big* eater when we was kids. Ate anything and everything. When we was eleven he used to eat a fly for a nickel ... ate a grasshopper for a dime.

* * * * *

Because you don't worry about *normal* things, like what the Jets are gonna do about Joe Namath's knees, think about that. You get yourselves into every weirdo worry that ever was.

* * * * *

Archie:	What've you two got goin' here? And don't tell me it's some kind of work—my heart couldn't take it!
Mike:	This is something we believe in, Archie. Remember, "Man does not live by bread alone."
Archie:	*You* sure don't. Not unless it's wrapped around ham, salami, baloney, liverwurst ... no wonder you're a meathead!

Archie: Why't you ask me an intelligent question?
Mike: I didn't want to confuse you.

* * * * *

Archie: It don't matter. All you gotta know is I wouldn't go near her with a ten-foot Polack!
Mike: Maybe she wouldn't go near *you* with a ten-foot Wasp!

* * * * *

What do I think? Well, when Gloria smiles with them straight teeth showing, I think of the three hundred and eighteen bucks it cost for the braces. When Edith smiles the same way, I think it's gotta be gas. As for you I think your underwear's too tight.

* * * * *

Mike: Come on, Arch. What's with the furnace?
Archie: Can't you see me workin' on this termostat here?
Mike: Well, hurry up. I'm sweatin' my brains out.
Archie: You done that when you were in diapers.

* * * * *

Archie: When this country needed Archie Bunker, he was there! Where were *you* in 1942?
Mike: I wasn't even born yet!
Archie: That's no excuse! Well, I was in Italy, fighting the Big One, one-hundred fifty-six missions over Europe, my group flew.
Mike: But you were in the ground crew.
Archie: Which, without them the planes couldn't never have took off!

Mike: What's the difference? Whoever it is, you won't like it. Nothing about us pleases you. You resent our attitudes, our politics, even our clothes. I don't think there's anything about us you agree with.

Archie: I agree with *that*!

* * * * *

Archie: You're some man, you are! She's gonna be out of here in a few minutes—and all you can say is you're too proud to stop her.

Mike: Whattya want from me, Archie. You and I are on the same side. Haven't I heard you say that a man's home is his castle and he's gotta be a king for it!

Archie: That's right. And when you get a home you can be a king. Until then *I'm* king, the princess is upstairs, and you're the pheasant that has to keep her here!

* * * * *

Mike: You can't call the police.

Archie: Why not? I'm a taxpayer. What's wrong with putting 'em to work once in a while?

* * * * *

Just what kind of animal did she bring into my house?

* * * * *

That's right. There was an argument and *she* left.

* * * * *

We lost a daughter, Edith, but we gained a meathead!

40

Archie: Miracle! My daughter's havin' a baby by you who can't even support a goldfish and she expects me to act like Moses just split the raging sea.

Mike: Archie, I gotta tell ya, my reaction was the same as yours.

Archie: It was, huh? When do you want to help me choke you?

Mike: I'm serious, Archie. I'm just as worried as you are.

Archie: That ain't good enough. I want you *more* worried than I am! When we was pregnant with Gloria, I not only had a job and an apartment, I had nine hundred and forty-two bucks in the bank!

Mike: I know, I know. This just happened. It was just one of those things.

Archie: Just one of "those" things, huh? It figures somethin' like this would happen the way you two was carryin' on around here—touchin' and squeezin' like you was pickin' fruit! You got a whole generation does nothing but think with its glands!

Mike: I tell ya, Archie, I was feeling guilty about it—but listening to you, I'm getting to feel damned proud!

*   *   *   *   *

Archie: All right, smart guy, you're proud! Now let me see you bank it. How are *you* gonna support a baby?

*   *   *   *   *

Whattaya mean, no baby? You didn't go and do something unlegal, you big dumb Polack?

41

How can he be our grandson? The only one he could
   belong to is Don Casanovsky up there. And *he* ain't
   no blood relative of ours.

* * * * *

Nothing you say tonight is gonna bother me, Meathead
   though you are. We've had a tiff or two in the past,
   Sonny Boy, and we ain't always seen nose to nose.
   But tonight I'm gonna show you what a real American thinks about living in the good old U.S. of A.

* * * * *

Put your money away! The dust from your pockets
   gets in my sinuses!

* * * * *

Archie: That don't mean I want to be kept in ignor-
   ance.
Mike: You mean you're changing your whole life
   style, Arch?

* * * * *

Archie: Well, I hope she don't run into no sales over
   there. (*Edith at market*) She's a sucker for
   specials. We still got fifteen pounds of nuts
   in the closet and we ain't even got a monkey.
Mike: Oh, I eat those nuts.
Archie: Well, you ain't long out of the trees.

* * * * *

If you're gonna ask the questions and answer 'em, too,
   whattaya need with us? You're a regular one-man
   family!

On hormone pills for Edith's menopause

Mike: Arch, what'd the doctor say?

Archie: Oh, too much . . . He said menopause ain't an easy thing to go through. 'Specially for nervous types.

Mike: So!

Archie: So he prescribed some pills here . . .

Mike: Oh, good.

Archie: I gotta take 'em twice a day.

Mike: What about *Ma?*

Archie: Oh, she's gonna be okay. He sends some pills for her too. Hormones. Which, by the way, these hormones are very hot stuff . . . They do a kind of alignment job on the glands. 'Cause right now your mother-in-law's glands don't know which way they're goin' and neither does she.

*   *   *   *   *

Archie: Lemme ask you a question. Let's say Gloria really means business and she stays away— say two, three months. What do *you* figure to do? I mean, this is a unique family group we got here—two parents and a son-in-law!

*   *   *   *   *

Mike: Shoot! Two more seconds and I'd have made it to freedom.

Archie: If it's freedom from me you're implying there —I got no bars on that front door.

*   *   *   *   *

Mike: Four years of school before I even begin to

43

make a living! It feels like forever!

Archie: Lemme tell ya' somethin', sonny boy, the same thought comes over me at least once a day. I tell you, Gloria, you married the laziest white man I *ever* seen.

* * * * *

Mike: But Arch, if there's no personal contact, there's no danger of further infection.

Archie: That's with regular germs. But them Polack bugs you got may be too dumb to know the rules and regulations. And if those germs of yours got any sense of all, they're poppin' out of you; right now lookin' for a better home.

* * * * *

Mike: It's you. The establishment. You—you property owners, with your twenty-four-inch TV's and your four-slice toasters and your ice-maker refrigerators. That's all you care about—what you got and how you can keep it.

Archie: You'd care about it, too, sonny boy, if you *had* anything. If you wasn't livin' offa me—without a pot to peel a potato in!

* * * * *

Mike: Who said anything about being an egghead—I just want to know something about society and people, so I can help them.

Archie: Here's two people—your mother-in-law an' me—help us—go to work!

* * * * *

You think he's a nice boy after he did what he did? Comin' in here, makin' suppository remarks about our country. And calling me prejudiced, while I was singin' "God Bless America," a song written by a well-known and respected Jewish guy. Milton Berlin.

* * * * *

Mike: So it's *their* fault you call 'em these names.

Archie: Like wops and coons and—

Mike: Okay, okay! Man, with your twist of mind, Archie, your brain must look like a pretzel.

Archie: And yours looks like what's inside a pretzel— nothing!

Mike: Touché.

Archie: I don't need none of your smart French swear words, neither.

* * * * *

Archie: If the kid was addressed to "occupant" . . . that's a mistake . . . but when he's dropped off Special Delivery for Michael Stivic—that's "guilty as charged"!

Mike: Why don't we all sit down and discuss this calmly?

Archie: All right. I'm gonna say this very calmly—get out!

Gloria: Daddy! Michael's right—it's obviously some kind of mistake.

Archie: Yeah—And *he* made it four years ago!

Archie: A Stivic talking to a Majeski. What could be better?

Mike: Archie, Majeski doesn't have to be Polish. He could be Russian or Jewish.

Archie: He ain't Jewish.

Mike: How can you be so sure?

Archie: His first name is John and those Hebes don't name their kids John.

Mike: What if he changed his name?

Archie: They just change their last names, not their first. That's how they know each other. Like two guys meet . . . "How do you do? My name is Smith—*Morris* Smith." Right away, they know! You see what I mean? Like—*Sol* Nelson. *Izzy* Watson . . .

Mike: *Abe* Lincoln.

Edith: I didn't know Lincoln was Jewish.

* * * * *

Mike: If you got any doubts about Father Majeski, why don't you ask him for his credentials?

Archie: Now, how can I do that?

Mike: Just walk up and say, "Father, can I see your cross?"

* * * * *

Archie: Oh, these sinuses are murder.

Mike: I wouldn't know. I never had a sinus condition.

Archie: You're lucky.

Mike: Is your head stopped up?

Archie: Yeah.

Mike: Well, that explains it!

* * * * *

Mike: (*practicing Spanish*) *Yo tengo cuarto.* I have a room.

Archie: You oughta finish that sentence. "I have a room for which I don't pay no rento." Whatta-

46

ya wanna learn yourself Spanish for, anyway? English is good enough.

Mike: Okay, Arch. When do you wanna start
learnin' *that*?

* * * * *

Mike: Hi, Arch. You look a little beat. What happened?

Archie: I was stuck in the subway for thirty-one minutes, that's what happened! Packed in like
sardines, we was, with no lights, *and no fans*,
and me standin' next to a three-hundred-
pound Eyetalian, half of which was pure garlic. What a city! Can't that Lindsay do nothin' right?

Mike: He turned Democrat.

* * * * *

Mike: Now I see what your idea of a free country is.
You're free to say anything *you* want, but if
anyone disagrees with you—they're either
meatheads or they get thrown in jail.

Archie: That's right. Because this is America! Land
that I love . . .

* * * * *

Mike: What's my being Polish got to do with anything?

Archie: Nothin'. Except it's common knowledge . . . if
you took one of your random house samples,
you'd find that—on the average—what they
call your curb—people of the Polack persua-
sion lean toward what you might call a certain lack of drive—you know, personal initi-

47

tianative.

Mike: First of all, Archie, I'm proud of my heritage. And second, that's the most fallacious argument I've overheard.

Archie: Yeah, maybe so . . . but it's true.

* * * * *

Archie: Colds affect me different. Ever since the war. The big one. It was sleepin' in a damp tent did it to me. Sleepin' in a damp tent, marchin' around in and—

Mike: Awright, Archie, not the war routine again.

Archie: I didn't start it. She knows damn well I get sick as a dog in the winter because—

Mike: We all know, Archie. You get the only war-connected colds in the country.

* * * * *

ARCHIE
AND HIS PRESIDENT

Whether he's right or right.

Dear Mr. President, your Honor, Sir—As one of your
faithful constitutionals. Naw, that's not the right
word.

*   *   *   *   *

I personally don't agree with all the conflagration on
the college campuses—or them ecology nuts who only see disaster in this great country of ours ... We
come up off the mat before, when the goin' was
tough and I know so long as we all work together
this nation under God shall not diminish from the
earth.

*   *   *   *   *

"My regards to your Vice, Mr. Agnew, and special regards to Mrs. Nixon and Tricia who I know you wouldn't let drink water exceptin' the best."

* * * * *

Mike: The way Nixon works it, nobody can afford to buy anything!

Archie: Don't give me that. Ain't he took the exercise tax offa cars?

Mike: Yeah! I'd forgotten that. How many cars you gonna buy, Archie?

Archie: Lissen you—ain't he doin' his best to keep wages and prices down?

Mike: Yeah, Archie, but not profits and interest rates. Don't you see what he's doing? Nixon's controlling the little man and letting the big guys run wild.

Archie: He never gave himself a raise. He froze himself, too, didn't he?

Mike: Yeah, he must be freezing with $200,000 a year and three houses.

Archie: He needs all that money to make 'em trips to China and Russia. He knows what's best for this country.

Mike: If he knows what's best for this country, why is he coming back?

Archie: Because he's my President, and I want him back. And that's what I told the CBS guy today, that there was millions of real Americans just like me who believes in Mr. Nixon. And God believes in him, too.

Mike: You said that on television? God believes in Nixon?

Archie: Certainly. Don't Billy Graham play golf with him?

Mike: So what does that mean?

Archie: It means God believes in Nixon.

Mike: What are you saying, Nixon rules because of Divine Right?

Archie: Well, it's a damn sight better than your Divine Left!

* * * * *

Geez. He's always on makin' everybody nervous . . . signing stuff and giving away all them ball-points.

* * * * *

Oh, geez . . . you know Nixon's gonna open his mouth once too often and he ain't gonna have Archie Bunker to kick around no more.

* * * * *

Archie: Geez, what a lousy break!

Mike: You just got pre-empted, Arch. The President does that all the time.

Archie: Why don't he let somebody else talk?

* * * * *

Well, I'll tell you one thing about Richard Nixon. He keeps Pat home. Which was where Roosevelt should have kept Eleanor. Instead he let her run around loose till one day she discovered the colored. We never knew they was there. She told them they was gettin' the short end of the stick and we been havin' trouble ever since.

* * * * *

Mike: Archie, *when* are you going to stop with this "Commie" jazz? It's all over, Archie—the whole

53

	Red scare is kaput! Nixon is going to Peking remember?
Archie:	Yeah . . . well, he ain't there yet.
Mike:	What's that supposed to mean?
Archie:	Twenty, thirty years Mr. Nixon has been warning us pretty good about them atheistic Red Chinks—an' nobody's gonna tell me I just like that . . . the old signals is off and a billion enemies is now our friends! I tell ya' the President has somethin' up his sleeve.
Mike:	Sure, like recommending that they be admitted into the UN.
Archie:	Never! This country ain't never gonna sit down with a nation of Chink ping-pong players who don't believe in God!
Edith:	God believes in them!

* * * * *

ARCHIE ON VOTING

Two cheers for an
informed Electorate!

Whoopee! Youth is voting! "And a little child shall
lead them!" Whoever said that didn't know nothin'!!

* * * * *

What's wrong with this? It looks like representative
government to me. Salvatory—Feldman—O'Reilly
and Nelson. You got an Eyetalian, a Jew, an Irish-
man and a regular American. That's what you call
a balanced ticket.

* * * * *

Now, for instance, you got Feldman for treasurer.
That's perfect. Them people know how to handle
money, y'know what I mean? Then you got Salvatory
for District Attorney—to keep an eye on Feldman.
And let me tell you about them Eyetalians—when

you do find an honest one you really got something!
Then you got a Mick—O'Reilly—to make sure the
graft is equally distributed—and you get Nelson, an
American, to do the TV appearances, to make the
rest of them look respectable.

* * * * *

I'm from the college of hard knocks, sonny boy! I've
been everywhere where the grass grows green and
I've seen everything!

* * * * *

Archie: Furthermore. This Claire Packer and her
whole Progressive Party—are losers. Now, if
you wanna pick a winner—
Gloria: I'm not interested in picking a winner!
Archie: I knew that the day you married this guy.

* * * * *

Archie: I know one thing. The winner of this here
election is gonna be Assemblyman Floyd J.
Lundy—your distinguished incrumbent.
Mike: How can you be for Lundy? Look at his record. He's against school bussin' . . . He voted
down every pay raise for teachers and he's a
hawk on Vietnam.
Archie: A great American.

* * * * *

I ain't even gonna look at your Claire Packer. Just let
her come in, turn her broom around and fly right
out again!

* * * * *

'Cause I cherish my vote, like it says you're supposed

to do, an' I don't waste it on these little meatball elections! I save it for the "biggies." Like the Presidential, the Senatorial, the Governororial, the Mayorororial . . . and them school bonds, what do I care about them?

* * * * *

You better stop runnin' for public office and start runnin' for a husband, 'cause from where I sit you got some runnin' to do.

* * * * *

You ain't gonna sell me none of your pregressive pinko welfare ideas . . .

* * * * *

Edith and I are gonna vote and that's gonna cancel out their votes, so from this house you get zilch! . . . And not only that, but I'm gonna follow you'se into that neighborhood tonight and cover it like a fine tooth comb. I ain't lived around here for over thirty years for nothin'. These are my people. They know Archie Bunker. I'm gonna knock on every door and window and tell 'em to stick to their guns and vote for Lundy—will you quit breathin' on me. We'll see who's gonna win this election—Packer or Bunker!

* * * * *

Just raisin' the flag to let everyone know—including the foreigners—that this house sits on American soil.

* * * * *

Archie: Small potatoes. Ya gotta have a dozen Philadelphia lawyers to figure out them propositions anyway—and then you find out all yer votin' on is whether to spend three million dollars lowerin' the hedges around the Mayor's mansion!!

* * * * *

Edith: Oh, no. You didn't vote for that Nixon, Archie. It wasn't the Humphrey—Nixon. It was the Kennedy—Nixon.

* * * * *

Mrs. Jefferson: Mr. Bunker, you haven't voted since 1960?

Archie: Well, I musta had things to do!

Edith: Yes. Something was always coming up. Once he had to mail a letter—and once—

* * * * *

Claire: Let me put it to you as directly as I can, Mr. Bunker—I want the vote of yours tomorrow. You tell me—how do I get it?

Archie: Get about eight guys to tie me down and drag me down there, then stick red hot coals under my toe nails.

* * * * *

Claire: Do you think John Wayne or Senator Eastland will ever pay back the money we're giving them?

Archie: John Wayne!! You better be careful, lady!

Claire: How about the huge subsidies we're giving him so he can raise cattle for fun and profit! If that isn't welfare for the rich . . .

Archie: It isn't! It isn't!
All right! That did it! This political percussion is over as of here and now!

* * * * *

ARCHIE AND LIONEL

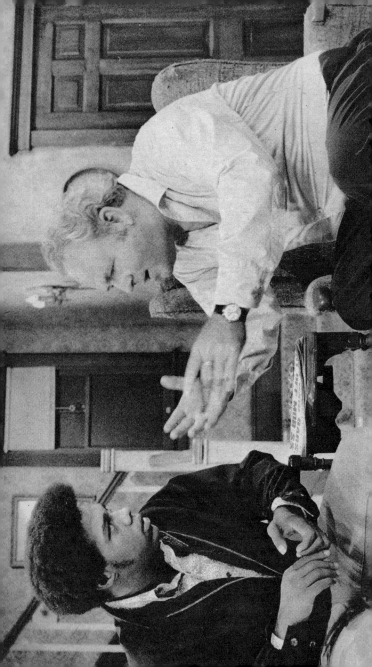

**One of *Archie*'s best friends is black
but *Archie* does not always get his message.**

Archie: Listen, Lionel—sit down—we've been friends
a long time, right?

Lionel: Right.

Archie: And it's on the basis of that friendship that
I'm going to ask you a favor.

Lionel: Sure.

Archie: You see, Lionel, Jim Bowman has sold his
house. And—well—the thing is—he's sold it
to one o' your coloreds.

Lionel: No!

Archie: Two doors away! Can you believe it!

Lionel: Does Mike know about this?

Archie: Sure he knows about it but he thinks twelve
percent of the whole neighborhood oughtta

be black.

Lionel: Oh really. If you follow that kind of thinking, eighty-eight percent of the Harlem Globetrotters ought to be white.

Archie: I never thought of that. Now, I've got nothing against your blacks, Lionel. A lot of them are very decent people, as you probably know.

Lionel: Yeah. So I've heard. But you just don't think that a black family would be more comfortable here, right?

Archie: Right.

Lionel: They'd be happier with their own kind.

Archie: Took the words right outta my mouth! Now, here's what I want you to do, Lionel. A group of intelligent and concerned people in the neighborhood are getting together to buy the Bowman house and we're gonna offer the colored a profit of $2,000. I want you to take the offer to them, Lionel. I'd do it myself, but for this job you got better credentials. I ain't askin' you to do this for nothing. If you pull it off there's twenty bucks in it for you!

Lionel: Twenty bucks for me! And I'm doing it for their own good, too!

Archie: Sure you are. What're they gonna do for recreation around here? There's no crap games, no pool halls. Not only that—there's not a chicken shack or a rib joint within miles of here.

Lionel: Lordamighty! What is we gonna do!

Archie: Wait a minute, Lionel, who's "we"?

Lionel: I gotta tell you something, Mr. Bunker, it's my family that bought Mr. Bowman's house and we're gonna keep it. We like it here. We like the house, we like the neighborhood, and I know we're gonna get along just fine with

64

the neighbors.

* * * * *

Archie: Let me ask you somethin' there, Lionel. When you started doin' odd jobs in the neighborhood, one of the first guys to throw some work your way—hey, by the way, didja fix the TV?

Lionel: Sure did, Mr. Bunker.

Archie: Here, let me give you something. Put that in your pocket.

Edith: Cheaper than a repairman, believe me.

* * * * *

Archie: Leave him alone, he's got no business picketing the military. They've been real good to your people—gettin' 'em off the streets, givin' 'em three squares a day, all them fancy uniforms...

Lionel: ... allowing them to die in Vietnam.

Archie: Yeah, well, Lionel. Ya gotta take the bad with the good.

* * * * *

Archie: Why didn't you just go out and jog along?

Lionel: Well actually I thought about that too. But let me ask you a question, Mr. Bunker. If you were walking down the street at seven o'clock in the morning and you saw a black kid running all by himself in this neighborhood—what would you think?

* * * * *

Lionel: He says you were both coming out of the

house at the same time and you saw each other and then *you* suddenly went right back inside.

Archie: Yeah, I forgot my lunch.

Lionel: But you came out a second later with nothing in your hand.

Archie: It was in my coat. Keep a hot lunch next to the body, it stays hot. Don't forget that, Lionel—that's good advice.

Lionel: How'd you like to meet Dad this afternoon, Mr. Bunker?

Archie: I'll tell ya, Lionel . . . I got a theory about neighbors, people livin' close together and all . . . It ain't a very fancy theory, but it's all mine. Lionel—Familyarity breeds content!

Lionel: That's a profound one, Mr. Bunker.

Archie: And it's got nothin' to do with color, neither.

Lionel: Oh, I know that, Mr. Bunker!

Archie: Because when it comes to the color of a man's skin—

Lionel: You're color blind!

Archie: No, I can't exactly say that! But I take 'em as I find 'em, Lionel. The one thing I ain't is prejudiced.

* * * * *

Lionel: There wouldn't be no problem about you coming over to our place. My dad's out at work.

Archie: No, I couldn't do that, Lionel. Not that *I* wouldn't go to your house like a shot. But I got other people coming over—guys from the plant. They might not be so broadminded as me. You know what I mean?

Lionel: Oh, I know what you mean.

Archie: I wouldn't want your family to be upset.

66

Lionel: Oh, listen, if that's worrying you, I could sneak you in and you could set in the back of the room.

Archie: Lionel, until you people learn to be serious, you ain't never gonna get ahead.

Lionel: Oh, I'll sure try to change, Mr. Bunker.

* * * * *

Archie: Lionel, we're friends, ain't we?

Lionel: And neighbors! We live right next to each other.

Archie: Yeah. Yeah. I know all about that. But gettin' back to bein' friends, I need your help.

Lionel: You got somethin' heavy for me to carry, Mr. Bunker?

* * * * *

Archie: Look at this—what's he doing with an Eyetalian name? I mean, how come a colored guy got a name like D'Angelo?

Lionel: Gets confusing, doesn't it? You know, there's a lot of black people named White and a lot of white people named Black. Why, just the other day I was delivering some cleaning to a a family named Rockefeller—

Archie: Black?

Lionel: No, white. Sometimes it works out just right.

* * * * *

Archie: Hold it, Lionel! I know how sensitive you people are, and don't be getting offended, but we got a problem here. So regardless of race, creed or color—I'd like you to leave.

Lionel: I'm not offended, Mr. Bunker, 'cause the way

you asked me meets every requirement of the Fair Employment Practices Act! 'Bye.

* * * * *

Lionel: This agent came over. He said he was questioning all your close friends.

Archie: Close friends?

Lionel: Well, I guess they slip up once in a while.

Archie: Yeah. Now what'd the investigator ask you and what'd you answer?

Lionel: Well—he asked if we thought you were a loyal American; if you took more than a social drink; whether you had many friends; do you read much; had we heard you discuss politics . . . you know, the usual.

Archie: And you answered?

Lionel: Let's see, I believe it went . . . "Yes, No, No, No, Yes, Perhaps . . ."

Archie: Hold it, hold it! How'm I supposed to follow *that*? Now—give it t'me straight, Lionel— how'd it go?

Lionel: Actually, there was nothing to it. We know what you are. And we told him.

Archie: Well now, that's better. Why didn't ya say so?

Lionel: We talked up real good, Mr. Bunker. Said you were a fine citizen.

Archie: Atta boy, Lionel.

Lionel: We told how you were one hundred percent behind the Constitution!

Archie: I couldn't said it better myself.

Lionel: One hundred percent behind Civil Rights!

Archie: Civil—?

Lionel: One hundred percent behind the Black fight for freedom!

Archie: Hahhh??

Lionel: You *are* for Black Freedom, aren't you?

Archie: Now, wait a minute, Lionel—

Lionel: It won't matter! We *said* you were. The family and me, we'd do anything to help you out, Mr. Bunker.

Archie: You told that to the G-man?

Lionel: Oh yeah! Between friends—what's a few white lies?

* * * * *

Archie: Lionel, can't you work any faster than that?

Lionel: No, Mr. Bunker. The minute you leave my side I slows down. We does our best work with an overseer watchin'.

Archie: Well, we ain't got one of them, Lionel.

Lionel: You got a whip, Mr. Bunker? That might help.

* * * * *

Archie: Because he's our material witness, and he shouldn't be seen.

Mike: You mean because he's black?

Archie: I never said nothing like that!

Lionel: You want me to hide in the woodpile, Mr. Bunker?

* * * * *

Archie: Hey, by the way, that's a pretty nifty, quiet-looking suit you got on there. Where'd you get it?

Lionel: Up in Harlem. I got two more, but one's in yellow with stripes, the other one's in purple with checks. You know, for when I'm with my people.

* * * * *

Archie: I'll tell you where he's sensitive, Lionel—in his tochas.

Lionel: Where?

Mike: It's a Yiddish word. It means—

Lionel: Oh, I know where it's at. I was just wonderin'—What's with the Jewish words, Mr. Bunker?

Archie: I hear them. We got a couple of Hebes working down the building.

Lionel: Does he use them very often?

Archie: I told ya', I work with a couple of Jews.

Lionel: Beggin' your pardon, Mr. Bunker, you wouldn't happen to be one of them, would you? There you are, Mr. Bunker. Now you oughta' be proud that you're Jewish.

Archie: But I ain't Jewish.

Edith: I didn't know you was Jewish.

Archie: What the hell are you talking about? You, of all people, *know* I'm not Jewish.

Edith: You are talking with your hands.

Lionel: See, the Jews tend to be emotional.

Archie: I'm going to tell you just once more—I'm not a Jew.

Lionel: Yes, sir, Mr. Bunker. But even if you are, it don't change things between you and me. I ain't gonna' kick nine years of friendship over a thing like that.

* * * * *

Archie: You got a cousin on the police force? Lionel, I didn't know that.

Lionel: Yeah, well, he's the white sheep of our family.

* * * * *

Lionel: Yeah, I know him. He's what we call an Oreo cookie.

Archie: Oreo cookie?

Lionel: That's right. Black on the outside and white on the inside.

Archie: I'm glad you liked him, Lionel. He struck me as a decent guy, too.

* * * * *

Archie: We got too many spray cans in the bathroom, Edith. I told you that before.

Edith: Yeah. Last week I reached for the liquid hairnet and sprayed my head with the room deodorizer. All day long I reminded myself of the great outdoors!

Archie: How do you people handle the spray problem, Lionel? I keep readin' about six families in an apartment, twenty people sharin' a bathroom.

Lionel: It's only four families and sixteen people, Mr. Bunker. And what we do is we shove our spray cans onto special shelves. So, what you could do is—shove yours.

* * * * *

Lionel: Oh, I'm used to him by now. You know his latest kick? Asking me what I'm going to be when I get out of college. He likes to hear me say—"Ah'm gonna be a 'lectical ingineer."

Mike: Why do you say it?

Lionel: Give the people what they want, man. How else do I get to become an electrical engineer?

* * * * *

ARCHIE ON CHARITY

**Charity begins at home—
and sometimes never leaves there!**

(On refusing clothes for charity drives)

Listen, that's the trouble with this country—too many handouts. Today every bum and his brother is collecting welfare, which is just another way of picking *my* pocket. Well, if he's gonna pick my pocket, it ain't gonna be in *my* suit.

* * * * *

Lady, you wanna stoop this conversation down to the gutter level, that's your derogative. But you ain't sellin' me on your pinko welfare give-away program.

* * * * *

I'm sick and tired givin' away hard-earned money to a
   bunch of families I ain't even related to—and
   wouldn't be related to me for complexionary rea-
   sons. If you know what I mean.

* * * * *

I'm saying I can't afford to make no donations to no
   Catholic charities. If you need the money that bad,
   wire the Pope! He's got more money than God!

* * * * *

Them big companies are gonna pay back every cent
   we give 'em. But the government ain't gonna get
   nothing back from those welfare moochers—unless
   it goes into the used Cadillac business!

* * * * *

Gloria: Look, Ma did something nice for Amelia, now
         Amelia's doing something nice for Ma.
Mike: Yeah—she earned that cape.
Archie: In the first place, *earnin'* is hardly your sub-
         ject, sonny boy, and, in the second place this
         ain't earnin's it's *charity*, which is something
         Archie Bunker don't take from nobody in the
         third place!
Mike: What charity? It's a gift, it isn't largesse,
         Arch.
Archie: I ain't sayin' it's largesse, smallesse or no'
         kinda esse. If I want my wife to have a fur—
         I'll buy her a fur.
Edith: Oh, Archie, will you?
Archie: No!

* * * * *

Mike:	I thought you didn't want to take charity.
Archie:	Well, I don't.
Mike:	It's a check from the insurance company, that's what it is, and if you think insurance companies give charity, you're dumber than I gave you credit for.
Mike:	It's Russ de Kuyper's money, because it was *his* cape that got damaged. So how can you honestly keep that three hundred dollars?
Archie:	The same way a lot of people make millions of dollars and pay no taxes! Like ... for instance Ronald Reagan there.
Mike:	Wait a second— You're throwing that example up to me?
Archie:	Certainly. That's the way the system's suppose to work. And Ronald Reagan knows how to work it.
Mike:	I was the one who told you about Ronald Reagan and you bawled the hell outta me for besmirching the name of a great governor.
Archie:	So! Don't do that no more! We got a certain way of doin' things here in the U.S. of A.... and givin' three hundred dollars back to a man who don't need it is like goin' against everythin' this country stands for.
Mike:	If that's what this country stands for, then the people have been devalued, not the dollar!

* * * * *

ARCHIE
AND THE FREAKS

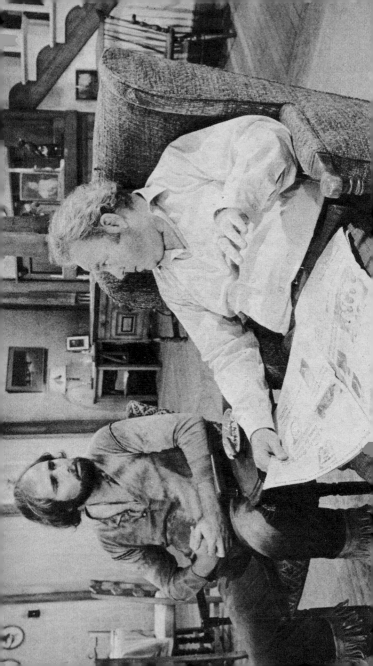

(To long-haired friend of *Mike* and *Gloria's* at the door.) All right, who and what is this, and why is it here?

Mike: Archie, you remember Paul Goodrow from Boston. He was my best man at the wedding.

Archie: Oh, yeah. I remember *him*. Who's this?

Mike: That's him.

Archie: You? You're that nice kid with the neat hair and the nice suit?

Mike: We wanted to tell you that we've invited Paul to stay tonight.

Archie: You hear that, Edith? *I* pay the mortgage and *he* sends the invitations.

* * * * *

Gloria: Paul is not weird! Besides, you used to *like* him.

Archie: I liked him when he was a clean-cut engineering student who wanted to build bridges and banks. Now he looks like somebody who wants to blow them up.

* * * * *

You let some of these freaks stay one night, they take a month.

* * * * *

Paul: Robin's my old lady.

Edith: This young girl is your mother?

Archie: No, Edith, she ain't his mother—because if she *were* his mother she'd be wearing a wedding ring on the third finger of her left hand which, if you'll allow me to point out, this girl is not!

Paul: No, we're not legally married if that's what you mean.

Archie: That's *exactly* what I mean.

Gloria: So they're not legally married. They happen to be very much in love.

Mike: That's right, Archie. And it's love that counts!

Archie: When it comes to stayin' overnight in *this* house it's marriage that counts! That love business may be okay in some places, but I'll have you know this is a Christian home!

* * * * *

Archie: What's that smell?

Gloria: Robin burning incense. Isn't it lovely?

Archie: Well, my life wouldn't be empty without it.

82

Smells like a house of ill refute, if ya ask me.

*   *   *   *   *

Let me tell ya something, kid. When you grow up, you'll learn there's more to life than being happy.

*   *   *   *   *

Archie: Robin, huh? What *does* she do, chirp? I mean, how does she communicate to people?
Paul: She thinks words are a waste of time. She speaks with her eyes.
Archie: Let me hear the Gettysburg Address. (*Robin crinkles nose.*) I think she said "no." Or was that the Gettysburg Address?

*   *   *   *   *

Archie: Narrow-minded's got nothing to do with it. Nobody stays outta wedlock under *this* roof.
Paul: We took vows, too.
Archie: But not in church, so God didn't hear them. You're not married in the eyes of God.
Paul: I thought God is everywhere.
Archie: He is.
Paul: Then He was there when we took our vows.
Archie: But He wasn't listening. Not without the license.

*   *   *   *   *

Archie: What're they doin'?
Mike: Transcendental Meditation.
Archie: What kinda freak thing is that?
Gloria: It's their way of removing themselves from this hostile environment.
Archie: I got a better way. The front door.

Lissen, I gotta get to bed. You kids swear t'me everything'll be kosher, they can stay over. Dormitory
style. Girls up there, men down here.

* * * * *

Archie: My mind's just as open as yours is, little girl,
except naturally when it's closed 'cause the
facts of the case is already known t'me.
Edith, this here is a Commie plot to under-
mine us just as sure as I'm standing here!
"...a place for the high school drop out, the
teenage runaway, that will provide free food,
free medical attention, free aid for V.D." See,
Edith?

Edith: VD? Don't rush me...I know it's someone's
initials.

Archie: Ask a question of a dingbat, get a dingbat
answer! Go fix dinner, will ya?

* * * * *

Now lemme tell ya about this. You spend time raising
money for things like this—you ain't gonna help
drop-outs and runaways—you're just gonna make
new ones.

* * * * *

Archie: I'll tell you what's *really* wrong with them
drop-outs today. They got no gratitude. Just
look what they got here! The greatest country in the world! The highest standard of
living! The biggest Gross Natural Product!
Whatta them young freaks want from us,
anyway?

Mike: Peace.

Archie: *One* thing they haven't got—and right away they drop out.

Mike: How about pure air? Clean water? Non-contaminated food? Confidence in government...

Archie: All right, all right! I didn't say we was perfect! This is the *United* States of America, not the *Perfect* States of America! All them freaks can do is tear the country down! Where are their solutions? Look, lemme tell ya somethin' that'll solve all o' their problems. Just let all o' them drop-outs, and them welfare incipients, an' them people trainin' for jobs they ain't never gonna get—let all o' them get off the public money—and you'll see how fast this country'll turn around. You'll have pure air and clean water comin' outta your ears.

* * * * *

Gloria: How can Daddy send them away like this, Ma? I'm so mortified.

Mike: Just because he's against people openly expressing their love for each other.

Edith: It ain't that. He just don't want them expressing it in a sleeping bag in the middle of his room.

* * * * *

Archie: Can't get away from them big deals for one night, huh, Eddie? Hear that, Mike? No wonder he's got the world by the short ones!

Mike: What is the thing you do best, Mr. Frazier?

Eddie: Breakin' the backs of my competitors and stompin' their faces in the dirt.

Archie: *That's* somethin' them drop-outs won't teach ya!

ARCHIE ON JUSTICE, CRIME AND PUNISHMENT

They pick jurors like your mother 'cause they don't know too much . . . People like your mother gotta be unpartial 'cause they got no subconceived notions.

* * * * *

I didn't insult the Defense Attorney. I just told him what I thought of pinko, bleeding-heart lawyers who get sentimental over killers.

* * * * *

It's a proven fact that Capital Punishment is a known detergent for crime.

* * * * *

If society is at fault that we got killers running around murdering innocent people, then it's simple. We turn the killer loose, give him a pension for life and shoot the rest of the city.

They put your mother in Superior Court? I hate to
even think what they're putting in the regular
courts!

* * * * *

Listen, Edith, I agree with ya that ya can't go around
discussing the case with strangers—but when it
comes to your own flesh and blood husband—

* * * * *

Of *course* he didn't come right out and say "Go home
and tell your husband." He takes that for granted.
It's a tactic understanding.

* * * * *

I *never* kept *nothing* from you. Why—I even told you
my secret vow from the Lodge. I could get black-
listed if the brothers found out I told you that.

* * * * *

The point ain't the Lodge vow, anyway. The point here
is the marriage vow. Don't you remember those
sacred words, Edith? For better or for worse, in
secrets and in health till death do us part?

* * * * *

Archie: Let me ask you something, buddy boy. Suppose you came home some fine day and find
your wife's throat has been cut . . . you mean
to say you wouldn't be itching to fry that
guy?
Mike: No, what's the use of that?
Archie: You see the kind of guy you married? A fiend

90

	comes in and kills you and this jellyfish won't lift a finger to help.
Mike:	If I *did* kill the murderer, would it bring Gloria back?
Archie:	No, but it wouldn't send her further away neither!
Mike:	Archie, an eye for an eye isn't the answer. The problem rests with society.
Archie:	So it's society's fault again, eh? Are you gonna tell me that society came in here and murdered Gloria?
Edith:	We don't even know any Society People.

* * * * *

Mike:	The way those Puerto Ricans are caged in those slums . . . it's no wonder the tension just builds and builds.
Archie:	Let 'em get out, then. Nobody's asking them to stay there.

* * * * *

It's an open and shut case. Two witnesses see this Martinez coming home, one witness sees him go into his apartment, and the rest is simply induction. He finds his old lady in there with another spic, whips out his switchblade—and Zap!—he sends him to that Big Taco Stand in the Sky!

* * * * *

(*Reading in the newspaper*) "The jury in the Martinez trial was sent back to continue deliberations today after the judge refused to accept a split decision. It is understood that one lone juror is blocking a unanimous verdict." Lone juror, huh? They

91

should have made it Lone Dingbat.

* * * * *

Archie: What's to say? Except that your mother's still throwing a monkey wrench into the halls of justice. What they ought to have are professional jurors.

Mike: What d'you mean professional?

Archie: People who are trained to sit on a jury.

Mike: That's crazy.

Archie: It's not so crazy as what you got now. You got a judge who spends half his life in school —after which he spends years as a lawyer, then a lower judge, then an upper judge, until he finally works his way up to a Superior Court. But does he get to decide who's innocent or guilty? No—that decision's made by four salesmen, three bank tellers, two plumbers, a seamstress, and a dingbat!

* * * * *

I'll tell you what I see. I see me suffering here for two weeks—living off dried squid—while you're out wasting the taxpayer's money trying the wrong guy!

* * * * *

ARCHIE
ON BEARING WITNESS

Archie: That's right, and I didn't see it, 'cause if you see somethin' you're a witness, and I don't wanna be a witness, so I didn't see nothin'.

Mike: Arch, if you saw anything, it's your duty as a citizen to come forward and be a witness.

Archie: That's great for your students and your unemployed, which for you is one and the same. But I'm a workin' man. I don't get paid if I show up for work absent.

Mike: Listen to that reasoning, will ya? I'll do the right thing—if they pay me!

Archie: Lemme tell you somethin'! Do you know what you gotta go through if you're a witness? You gotta put on a shirt and tie, drag myself downtown and hang around till the case comes up, which you never know when. And by the time it does, you forget what you was gonna say, and the other lawyer makes a monkey outta you! And it all goes on your record!

Mike: So you're saying because of a little incon-

	venience—you don't want to get involved.
Archie:	Lemme explain somethin' to you—shut up!

* * * * *

Archie:	Forget the truth, I'll tell you what happened ... We went into the deli, and bought a six pack and some cigars. And Old Man Schneider was waitin' on us, groanin' about his aches and his pains, the worst hypochondri-jerk in the neighborhood, and meathead here had to ask him somethin' stupid.
Mike:	All I said was—"How are you?"
Archie:	That's the one. That opened up the hydrant. And I couldn't shut him off. I get a complete medical report.

* * * * *

Me bein't there don't prove nothin'. I was in Italy durin' the war, that don't mean I've seen Musselini.

* * * * *

Gloria:	Michael, how can you be so certain Daddy saw the mugging?
Mike:	Gloria, will you stay out of this?
Archie:	She makes sense. A man oughtta listen to his wife.
Edith:	Archie ... ?
Archie:	Dry up.

* * * * *

Mike:	Archie, you know you saw it.
Archie:	Don't tell me what I know. You don't even know what you know, schoolboy! That's why

you're a meathead!

* * * * *

Edith: I know you'll do what's right. Just ask yourself—what do you feel in your heart?

Archie: Heartburn. Edith, get me some bicarb.

* * * * *

Mike: And you saw that. Boy—if I were you, I
couldn't live with myself.

Archie: You ain't livin' with yourself—you're livin'
with me.

* * * * *

It ain't lyin' when you're tryin' to protect your family!
If anything happened to me, the meathead here
couldn't keep you in bubble gum!

* * * * *

Mike: It was just an ordinary mugging, wasn't it?
Well, wasn't it?

Archie: No! It wasn't. It was the most unordinary
mugging I ever seen! Did you ever seen an
ordinary mugging with a big car comin'
screechin' up to the curb?

* * * * *

Br—I'll tell you why I couldn't have seen no actual
muggin ... 'cause I was facing this way. And posi-
tion is nine-tenths of the law, right?

* * * * *

ARCHIE AND
SURVEILLANCE

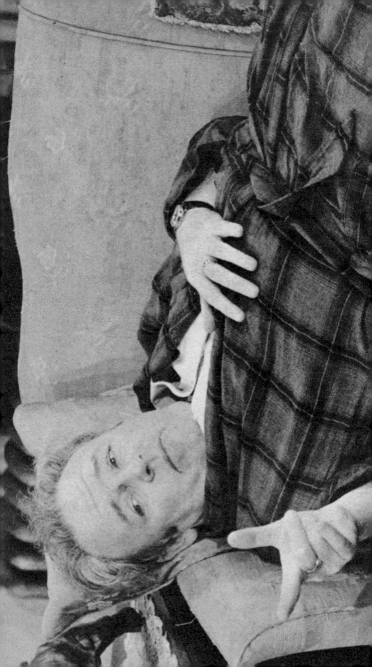

He loves his neighbor—except when the government's asking questions about him.

Oh, Larry Grundy from across the street? Yeah, well, we can't help bunkin' into each other now and then . . .

* * * * *

I got a *lotta* best friends! Some o' them I don't even hardly know!

* * * * *

He's talkin' about some old war like 1812 . . . you know, the one between the States.

* * * * *

There, you see? No shelves, no books. I think the guy's
okay.

* * * * *

Let's see . . . Politics—I think I remember Larry sayin'
—"Mayor Lindsay is a crumb!" That's okay. I've
heard him say, "American, love it or leave it." What
could be better than that?

* * * * *

Oh, let's see. He belongs to our bowling team. The
American Legion . . . Knights of Columbus. But I
don't think you ought to hold that last one against
him. Because Grundy's one of the good Catholics.
He don't bother with it.

* * * * *

Youse two just sit there and keep your mouth shut!
Watch your government doin' secret work! And
learn something about democracy in action!

* * * * *

Hold it, Lar . . . Your uncle! How much do you really
know about that uncle of yours? He went to Europe
one year!

* * * * *

Listen, Larry, you say you don't know what the in-
vestigation's about, I buy that. You say you ain't
got nothin' to hide. I buy that! But I ain't the guy
you gotta sell. Now listen—This FBI guy's gonna
start wonderin' if I don't get in there . . . So you go
home, take it easy . . . Kinda lay low. Don't call me

up, I'll get in touch with you—

*   *   *   *   *

Brad-
ford: Right. Now, as to his use of intoxicants. How
           would you describe Mr. Grundy's drinking
           habits?
Archie: He seldom buys.

*   *   *   *   *

What's he drink? Tab beer mostly . . . But don't go by
   me. Like I said before, we bunk into each other now
   an' then, but there ain't no real connection between
   us.

*   *   *   *   *

Oh, you should've seen him in the kitchen, little girl—I
   mean nervous, and where there's fire, there's bound
   to be smoke!

*   *   *   *   *

Certainly I'm innocent, Edith. But of what?

*   *   *   *   *

Edith: I don't see nobody.
Archie: Of course not, Edith! Them FBI guys is ex-
           perts at keeping hidden.
Edith: Then how do you know they're watching?
Archie: If they wasn't watching, you could see 'em.
           If you can't see them, then they're watchin'.
           See?
Edith: Oh!
Archie: Hey, look at that there. I ain't never seen

that car on this block! That could be them! Huh, Edith!

Edith: You mean—the one with the lady and the three children getting out?

Gloria: That could be them, Daddy! I hear they're masters of disguise.

Archie: Well, they are—they're tricky.

*   *   *   *   *   *

Benedict Arnold was an admiral, but he was as subversive as a termite.

*   *   *   *   *

Wounded in action!? You was wounded openin' a beer can in the PX.

*   *   *   *   *

Stifle yourself, Edith! I don't need to dress up like no tin soldier to remind me I'm an American.

*   *   *   *   *

Oh, you're nuts, Grundy. The kid's stupid, but he ain't dangerous.

*   *   *   *   *

(Into a supposedly bugged room)

I want you all to know that whatever the FBI does is okay by me! If they're sneakin' around, listenin' and watchin', it's for our own benefit. I got no secrets from J. Edgar Hoover—a great Commie killer. And remember you heard it from Archie Bunker.

*   *   *   *   *

Edith: Wasn't that nice of the Jeffersons? Giving you such a nice recommendation?

Archie: Any more recommendations like that, and you can mail my new Fruit of the Looms to San Quentin!

*   *   *   *   *

Archie: That's right, *Safe* City. Where the minorities don't outnumber the majorities. They got TV monitors in the lobbies, special locks, twenty-four-hour guards and a twelve-foot wall around the whole thing.

Mike: You're gonna move to San Quentin?

*   *   *   *   *

Mike: Hey, Arch, listen to this. We've been doin' some research on some of the people who've been investigated by the government in the last year.

Gloria: Yeah, Daddy, you're in good company. Congressmen, Senators, and Supreme Court Judges . . .

Edith: Did you hear that, Archie? How about that?

Archie: Yeah, well . . .

Mike: That's right, Arch, and Dr. Spock, Huey Newton, Father Berrigan and Abbie Hoffman . . . Jerry Rubin, Rap Brown, Eldridge Cleaver.

THROUGH ARCHIE'S PINKO-COLORED GLASSES

What sermon? That was Socialist propaganda, pure and simple. And don't look at me like that. And I'm not sittin' still for no preacher blamin' me for all this here breakdown in law and order. The cause of it is all them sob sisters like the Reverend Felcher. All the bleedin' hearts and weepin' Nellies like you two!

* * * * *

It's them liberals, sittin' around dreamin' up causes, a dozen at a clip! Like f'instance—giving the kids free shots for VD. It's positively disgusting! When I was a kid you had to be in the Army to get free shots for VD.

* * * * *

And nice to meet you, Miss Packer—so as I can give you the piece of mind I've been wantin' to give you. If you liberals keep gettin' your way—we're all gonna hear one big loud flush. The sound of the U. S. of A. goin' straight down the toilet!

* * * * *

Why is it, you liberals, no matter what subject you talk about, always leads to that? You guys got more ways for the world to end than a dog's got fleas!

* * * * *

Nice. The guy comes into my house, dressed like a famous white man. Sits in my chair here, and imagine his makin' a pinko (peace) sign like that . . . on Christmas Day.

* * * * *

Cousin Maude: It was a choice of Civil Rights or Civil War.

Archie: We got Civil War—riots in the streets.

Maude: Caused by Poverty and Un-employment.

Archie: Caused by Roosevelt the original creepin' Socialist!

Maude: He pulled this country out of the Depression.

Archie: And right into World War II.

Maude: When he won as Commander-in-Chief.

Archie: General MacArthur won the war and Roosevelt fired him.

Maude: That was Truman.

Archie: Under sealed orders from FDR!

Maude: What?

Archie: A well-known fact—and he sold us out to Joe Stalin at Gibraltar.

Maude: They met at Yalta!

Archie: He sold us out there too! Handed Europe over to the Russkies on a silver platter! And that's that.

Archie: Petey, the guy with the strawberry boil on the end of his nose, that he was always covering up with talcom powder. Petey, the white-nosed Commie.

Larry: Petey? A Commie?

Archie: That's right. Remember, that night we was all talkin' about Spiro Agnew—and what did Petey say?

Larry: He didn't say nothin'.

Archie: On orders from you know who. That's how them Commies work. And you're his friend.

* * * * *

Archie: I don't want to have nothin' to do with the red Reds or the yellow Reds. It's their fault we're sick in the first place. Who do you think we got the Asiatic Flu from? The Eskimos? You put our bugs under a microscope and ten to one, they got slanty eyes!

Mike: Don't change the subject! I'm talking about art.

Archie: Which is just an excuse for Commie infliteration! Now we're playing footsie with China! You know what's gonna happen? Them Red Chinks will be comin' over here, openin' up laundries and puttin' our good American Chinks out of business.

Okay. I just learned somethin'. I learned I don't like watchin' that Commie fairy tippy-toein' around in his panty hose, which is six sizes too small for him in the first place—and in the second place, too. It don't belong on American TV.

Mike: What are you talking about, Archie? Ed Sullivan himself had Russian Ballet Companies

111

on his program many times!

Archie: Well, let me tell you something, Sonny Boy
If Ed Sullivan had stuck with tap dancers,
he'd still be on the air today!

* * * * *

Mike: Art is a universal language. It has nothing to
do with politics. It's a way of bringing people
together, so that they can talk to each other.

Archie: There's only one way you can talk to a Commie, and that's to keep your mouth shut!

Mike: Archie, don't you believe in Cultural Ex-
change?

Archie: I don't believe in any one of them two words.
I go along with Walt Disney—rest his soul—
He hit them Commies where it hurt, when he
kept Khrushchev out of Disneyland.

Mike: It wasn't Walt Disney. It was the Chief of
Police. He was afraid Khrushchev would turn
Snow White to Rose Red!

Edith: I felt so sorry for him. After coming all that
way, he never even got to see Mickey Mouse
and Minnie and Goofy...

* * * * *

ARCHIE ON
BLOOD
AND TRANSPLANTS

don't like the idea of givin' blood without knowin' who's on the receivin' end . . . The difference is— some radical gets shot while he's trying to blow up a building, an' he needs a transfusion, he ain't gonna wind up with any of Archie Bunker's blood in him!

* * * * *

You think William Buckley's gonna give blood to some Commie punk what's just blowin' up a buildin'?

* * * * *

Archie: Fact is, little girl, blood is like everything else in life—you got your good and your bad. John Dillinger has bad blood.

Mike: John Dillinger?

Archie: He's arguing blood and doesn't know who John Dillinger was! You're over your head, sonny boy, get outta the argument.

* * * * *

Whaddaya mean my heart's like a pump? The heart's only the most emotional part of your body—anybody knows that. That's where your love and romance are kept. We're not machines yet, dammit.

* * * * *

You talking about transplants? 'Cause if you're talk-ing transplants you're gonna make my point for sure. First time out they put a woman's heart in a man's body. Right? So it's tough enough to get a man and a woman living together in the same house, never mind the same body! The heart was rejected. Case closed. Next case.

* * * * *

No sense in makin' a fuss. Little pint of blood, that's all. I don't think I'll bother with a sling.

* * * * *

That arm's thinner than this one now, ain't it? Of course it is! They drained too much outta this one. It's a wonder I was able to stagger back here at all.

* * * * *

How d'you know what they're doing when they've got you on that table? You go to a hospital nowadays and before you know it, they got you opened up and they're looking around inside to see what's any good. If they see anything they fancy—anything they like —snip, it's gone! It's in a bloody jar! "Hello! There's

116

a nice set of kidneys. They seem to work a hell of a lot better than mine. Here we go. Snip, snip." That's what them medics will do. Keep themselves alive at our expense.

* * * * *

When you gotta go, you gotta go. You go because *He* wants you. And *when* He wants you. And He don't want no quack doctors putting new hearts into you and keeping you here against His will. 'Cause it throws Him off his schedule. It throws Him all off. Now you do that to Him . . . throw His schedule off like that, and when you get up there . . . in Heaven . . . when you get up there you'll have no answer to Him, won't you? Because He'll want to know why you didn't come up when you were called. Why you were late. Why you ignored Him . . . And another thing. You'll have to answer to the guy whose heart you took down here. Can you imagine it? You've had to give back your new heart—what do you do? You go looking for your old one . . . But do you think you can find it? Do you think those doctors have taken care of it for you? Not on your life! They've thrown it in a pail—Your heart's in a pail and you're in Heaven with a hole in your chest.

* * * * *

Lionel: They get all confused, don't they? The goodie-goodie white liberals! Tell them we all come from the same God—tell 'em all men are brothers—and right away they think we all have the same blood.

Archie: Yeah . . .

Lionel: I mean, if they start bunging our blood into

117

	you white folks . . . who knows what might happen? You could all turn black.
Archie:	We couldn't!
Lionel:	Would you chance it?
Archie:	Not me! Not on your life.

* * * * *

Lionel:	Transplants. Bad business, unless of course, it's white on white—
Mike:	Lionel, cut that out.
Archie:	Yeah, don't disagree with him, Lionel. He only likes it when you have the same opinion as him.
Lionel:	I remember one of the first heart transplants they did. In South Africa, it was. Remember, they put the black heart in the white body? Now, talk about rejection! You just can't mix 'em up like that.
Archie:	You tell 'em, Lionel.
Lionel:	And even if that heart in South Africa wasn't rejected, the blacks don't have their civil rights down there, the way we all enjoy 'em up here, so can you imagine the black heart in a white body? I mean, for a start, the man wouldn't even know what public restroom to use.
Archie:	I never thought of that.

* * * * *

ARCHIE ON
COUSIN OSCAR, DEATH,
AND BURIAL RITES

**The *American Way of life, si!*
The *American Way of death, no!***

Almost noon, and that deadbeat is still sawing wood!

* * * * *

Oscar's about six years older'n me . . . and he was always this big hulkin' thing, with all that red hair and ear lobes big as apricots, and all them warts . . . and when we was kids he used to chase me in the grass and knock me down and sit on my face!

* * * * *

What's he need supplements for? The man eats more
than all of us put together. If he lived here regular,
it'd be over the hill to the poor house.

* * * * *

I'm gonna let that freeloader know right now that his
welcome has been outstayed. Mike, I want you to
run up them stairs and get Oscar outta bed. Tell
him t'get outta my pajamas and get his tail down
here.

* * * * *

His steak, huh! Put it back in the freezer. It's probably big enough for the four of us and we'll eat it
New Year's Eve. He won't have time for lunch, anyway, 'cause Cousin Oscar is leavin' here, in post and
haste.

* * * * *

Now get all that food off here, he'll eat anything in
sight. Family feelings can go just so far and then
you gotta grab the bull by the corns and heave-ho.

* * * * *

Well, he sat on my face again. Relatives in sixteen
cities and he's got to die in my attic!

* * * * *

Whitehead, spare me 'em stained glass answers.

* * * * *

White-
head: The casket, Arch. His home through eternity.

122

Archie: The man couldn't care less about a home when he was living. Now I gotta give him one through eternity!

* * * * *

Edith, you take care of Mrs. Jefferson. And there'll be people coming here, so try and get an apron on her. Make her look like a maid.

* * * * *

A death in the family and the whole woodwork opens up.

* * * * *

Mrs.
McNab: Mr. Bunker, do you think the funeral will be in the morning? I usually do my shopping in the morning.

Archie: Yeah, well, I'll keep that in mind. Maybe we could pass the market on the way.

* * * * *

In fifty years, he never worked a day. To him, nine to five was odds on a horse.

* * * * *

Still doin' it to me, ain't you, Oscar! Twenty bucks to get a house call from Kelly. Maybe four bucks to call Cousin Lou in Detroit. Another thirty bucks maybe just to get him picked up. Dead twenty minutes and you've cost me more'n fifty bucks already!

* * * * *

I got some real bad news for you. Cousin Oscar is dead
. . . Whaddya mean, "How's the weather in New
York?"

* * * * *

Okay, Whitehead, I know you thirteen years from the
Lodge. Now you're a Funeral Director. I remember
when you was an undertaker, Smitty the Sanitary
Engineer was a garbage man, Harry the Building
Maintenance Supervisor was a janitor—and Gus,
the Welfare recipient was just another bum outta
work.

* * * * *

Was Uncle Oscar's death very untimely, you ask? Well,
it was near lunch.

* * * * *

Are you telling me McNab laid out $926 bucks for
the dead? Edith collected for the Red Cross last
year. He gave her only a dime.

* * * * *

(*About caskets*)

Look, Whitehead, I know you thirteen years, so I'm
gonna talk plain. Can a guy buy such a thing as
used? You got any old floor models, demonstrators,
fleet jobs—things with nicks, scratches and tears—
whatever?

* * * * *

When Archie Bunker gives a funeral, people show up.

* * * * *

Archie: Edith . . . how much money do we have in our savings account?

Edith: Nine hundred and forty-one dollars, and eighty-one cents exactly!

Archie: How can we blow all o' that dough . . . And on a cousin that used to sit on my face.

Edith: We been through worse than this, Archie.

Archie: When?

Edith: Well, we been through things just as bad.

Archie: When?

Edith: Well—then we been kinda lucky, ain't we?

* * * * *

ARCHIE ON GOD, JESUS, AND THE CHURCH

Archie: "And the rib which Lord God had taken from man made He a woman and brought her unto the man. And Adam said this is now a bone of my bones and flesh of my flesh and shall be called woman because she was taken out of man." There it is in black and white! So we *didn't* crawl out from under the rocks and we *didn't* have tails, and we *wasn't* a bunch of monkeys neither, you atheistic pinko meathead you.

Mike: Archie, that was written in the dark ages. The whole idea of taking a rib out of Adam and making a woman—it's Mandrake the Magician time.

Archie: Edith! Did you hear what I heard? This meathead's comparing God with Mandrake the Magician. Can you believe it?

Edith: No. God is much better known.

* * * * *

Archie: Listen, I give up on you two! Maybe *you* came from monkeys and baboons, but *I* was made by God in His own image.

Mike: You mean God looks like *you*?

Archie: I didn't mean there was any exact resemblance. I mean he made us perfect like Himself, that's what I mean.

Mike: Perfect?

Archie: Yes, perfect . . . No, I don't mean perfect that way . . . I mean . . . I got faults, I'm not saying I ain't. None of us is perfect. What I mean is—He made us with—well—with four fingers and one thumb on each hand. He even thought of that, two hands. Because He knew one hand wasn't gonna be good enough. And He put them on the end of your arms where they'd be most handy . . .

Edith: That's why they're called hands, I suppose.

Archie: Will you stay out of this, Edith! God don't want to be defended by a dingbat.

*   *   *   *   *

He gave you the world and everything in it. All the kind of food you like to eat. He put them there for ya. Like your cows which turn themselves into your beef, and then your pig and your lamb. The thing I don't get is—what could you two possibly have against Him?

*   *   *   *   *

The Bible's full of wine. God ain't got nothing against a little drink to celebrate his Son's birthday with.

*   *   *   *   *

Oh, listen you, Meatheaded Atheist. They wouldn't

130

give you no holiday for fairy tales, would they? I mean the whole world celebrates the birth of that baby and everybody gets time off from work. If that ain't proof he's the son of God, what is?

* * * * *

Half a sermon was plenty. He said all he was gonna say.

* * * * *

Archie: (*on the Bible*) It's all facts right from the very beginnin', when God made the world in seven days.

Edith: Six days, Archie.

Archie: Seven, Edith!

Edith: No. On the seventh day He rested.

Archie: Maybe half a day, but the other half he was checkin' on what he done . . . And He made everyone the same religion—Christians. Which He named after His Son, Christian—or Christ for short. And that's how it was for years. One religion. Until they started splitting 'em up 'til all them other denumerations. But there's still only one true religion. His up there.

Mike: And, of course that's the only one you belong to, Arch?

Archie: I'd be pretty stupid not to, wouldn't I? . . . I tell you my heart goes out to a lot of guys I know. They spend all their lives belonging to one of 'em Anything Goes Religions. They raise their kids in it, they give money to it, they run dances for it . . . only to get up there someday and find out they was foolin' around with the wrong one all the time! It's sad, you know that.

131

(*Archie* discusses God with his black neighbor, *George Jefferson*)

Archie: Interestin', too. I mean how the black people went from worshippin' snakes and beads and wooden idols—all the way up to our God.

George: What do you mean, your God?

Archie: Well, he's the white man's God, ain't he?

George: That ain't necessarily so. What makes you think God isn't black?

Archie: Because God created man in his own image, and you'll note I *ain't black*.

George: Well, don't complain to me about it.

Archie: Look, you seen pictures of God, ain't ya? That dago artist painted him on that ceiling in Rome ... remember?

George: You mean that *white* dago artist painted him.

Archie: Every picture I ever seen of God, He was white.

George: Maybe you were looking at the negatives.

Archie: Wait a second. You say God is black. Now if he *was* black, that'd mean His Son was black, too—and you ain't telling me that *Jesus* was black!

George: Now you're catching on! It's been proven that Jesus was Ethiopian.

Archie: Look, you say he's an Ethiopian. The Presbyterians say he's a Presbyterian. But no matter what He was, He wasn't black.

* * * * *

Archie: Listen, you and me had this argument before over Jesus and I ain't going over old ground again. Jesus was white and so was Santa Claus.

George: Listen, Bunker—when I was a kid the guy who filled my stocking on Christmas Eve was black.

* * * * *

Jesus Christ is who's great, little girl. I know that long before them rock and roll freaks made Him a "superstar."

* * * * *

Jesus Christ don't want you turning *on* to him, sonny boy! He wants you comin' to him on yer knees, not wigglin' and jigglin' till your parts fall off.

* * * * *

Jesus Christ, Superstar! Your whole damn generation —we try to talk sense to ya, we take you to church —we teach you religion—and you give us back the Son of God like he's some "Englebum Hunkerdunk."

* * * * *

Archie: Whaddya bringing Him into this for?
Vicino: He sees everything. He knows everything we do.
Archie: Then how come you people are always running to confessions, tellin' him everything that happens?
Vicino: Now we're gettin' the truth. It's because I'm Catholic that you ain't helpin' me.
Archie: That ain't the truth. I'd say the same thing even if you belonged to the right church.
Vicino: Boy, was I wrong about the kind of guy you are. And to think my Rosa was gonna mention you in her prayers—

Archie: Listen, I can look after my own soul. Shoe-maker, you look after the other kind.

* * * * *

Archie: It ain't a question of sides. God is always on the side of right.

Mike: And we're always right.

Archie: Well, of course we are! You don't expect them Godless Gooks to be right, do you?

Mike: How can those Gooks be Godless, Archie, when God created them?

Archie: God *didn't* create them, smart guy! It was the devil what created *them*.

Mike: And who created the devil, I wonder.

Edith: I suppose it was God, huh, Archie, since He created everything?

ARCHIE AND SEX

Used to be, the daylight hours was for the respectable things in life.

* * * * *

Archie: In my day we used to keep things in their proper suspective. Take keepin' company, for instance. When your mother-in-law and me was goin' around together—two whole years it was—we didn't—I never—there was nothin' —I mean nothin'—not till the wedding night.

Edith: Even then.

* * * * *

Do you always have to be doing that? It's as if she was a hamburger?

* * * * *

First you laugh like you're comin' unglued, now you look like you're tryin' to swallow each other. What's

137

goin' on back there, anyway? And you don't need to draw me any diaphragms neither!

* * * * *

My God! They're a couple of guppies!

* * * * *

The Vice-President of the United States ain't nobody to be swappin' saliva over! I tell ya, the way you two carry on, one of these days, sure as I'm standin' here, you're gonna do yourselves an injury.

Gloria: Oh stop that, Daddy! Michael does more odd jobs around the house than you do.

Archie: Yeah. Like what he was *doing* with you when I came downstairs. That was an odd one all right.

* * * * *

Mike: You know, Archie, the whole thing with you about Paul and Robin—it's just one of your sex hang-ups.

Archie: I got no hang-ups at *all* about . . . that.

Mike: No hang-ups? You can't even say the word "sex."

Archie: I don't *use* four-letter words in front of women. There are certain subjects that should only be dealt with—in the privatcy of one's—upstairs.

* * * * *

That's tommycock and poppyrot!! I disagree with the whole diagnoses. Now listen to me good. All them exams has done is take your mind off everything else—so it figures, logicly, you been forgettin'

to do certain other things. Now—all you gotta do, at
the end of the day, is sit down with a pencil and paper and ask yourself, "Is there anything else I oughtta do before I go to sleep?" And then write yourself
a little note—you know, like a reminderandum!

* * * * *

Archie: You remember Gloria's honeymoon, don't
you, meathead? It was the same time you
was on your honeymoon.

Mike: Sure, I remember it, Archie. We checked into the hotel at Niagara Falls and went
straight up to the room. Gloria took a shower
while I got undressed. Then I—

Archie: All right. That's enough of that! And enough
with the pancakes, too. You're eating like the
Russians are marching up Queens Boulevard.

* * * * *

Archie: Say . . . uh . . . Jefferson, can I talk to you—
kind of private?

Henry: Sure, sure. What's up?

Archie: Well, it's . . . er, kinda delicate . . . There's
this, er, friend of mine who's run into some,
what you call, connubible difficulties . . . a
married man, but he—uhhh—

Henry: Can't make the scene?

Archie: I suppose you could put it that way—yeah.
Now, Henry—it's a well-known fact that you
people . . . that is, the men . . . you got this
sort of . . . prowress, with the members of the
opposite . . . A kind of special stanima . . . you
follow me?

Henry: Yes, I hear we're quite advanced in that department.

Archie: Right, right. And that's why I'm coming to you for help . . . er . . . for my friend.

Henry: Gosh, I don't know, Bunker. I mean if it were for you, okay . . . but it's such a well-guarded racial secret.

Archie: Aww, you can tell *me*. I mean, we're neighbors and practically friends, ain't we?

Henry: Yeah, practically.

Archie: Is it somethin' in that soul-food you people are always eatin'?

Henry: Well, shut my mouth!

Archie: No, no, don't shut your mouth, tell me.

Henry: But you hit it, right on the button!

Archie: I did?

Henry: And they say you people ain't instinctive. Well now that you all but guessed it, I might as well tell you. It's the . . .
. . . hog jowls.

Archie: Hog jowls . . . !

Henry: Shhhhhh!
Now some'll tell you hog jowls and hominy— "The Combination"—but I'd advise you to leave off the hominy. Hell, you take The Combination, you might as well *be* a black man!

Archie: Skip the hominy! Skip it! The hog jowls is plenty, anyway!

Henry: Well then, good, Bunker, you just try that now, maybe a jowl in the morning and a jowl at night and you'll be just fine.

Archie: Look, Jefferson, this wasn't for me. I got no problems.

Henry: Come, come, Bunker, you don't have to play that game with me, we're practically friends, ain't we?

Archie: But it ain't me, I tell ya. I'm a man!

Henry: 'Course you are, we don't recommend hog

140

jowls to women.

Oh, I almost forgot to tell you about the side effects.

Archie: Side effects?

Henry: Oh yeah. You might develop a sudden craving to shine shoes, or you might automatically start moving to the back of the bus. I heard of one extreme case where a man tap danced himself to death.

* * * * *

ARCHIE ON
THAT OTHER SEX

His heart is neither young nor "gay."

I never said a man that wears glasses is a queer. A man that wears glasses is a four eyes. A man that's a fag is a queer!

* * * * *

In them days Notre Dame was playing hard knocks football! No fat scholarships, none of them pet parties—and the players didn't all the time go around patting each other on the behinds!

* * * * *

I've listened to this boy for ten months now. I figure his pinko ideas, that's what they're stuffing him with in the schools now. The way he dresses—well, all the kids take from each other and one is crummier than the next. The sexual submissiveness? It don't matter whatever time of day or night—well, that's your dismissive society. But when they start besmirching the reputation of a great linebacker, a runner-up All-American, a real man, and I mean a *real* man . . . then we might as well just shut the doors of this country and hang a sign on it saying *Closed—Owner Gone Nuts.*

* * * * *

Edith: But they seemed like such a nice couple.

Archie: Nice couple of what? He ain't a he and she ain't she!

Edith: What do you mean, Archie?

Archie: Do you remember Richie Clifford from across the street who was always sittin' on the front steps knittin' sweaters?

Edith: Oh, yeah. He taught me how to cable stitch.

Archie: Yeah, Remember Schultzy's daughter, Maxene? The cab driver? The one they wouldn't let into the Teamster's Union?

Edith: Oh, you mean Butch!

Archie: Yeah, that's right.

Edith: Oh! You mean he's a—

Archie: Yeah!

Edith: And she's a—

Archie: Yeah! Tootie and Fruitee!

* * * * *

ARCHIE AND
THE MOVIES

'Cause they've gone too far in some of them movies—
some of them is nothin' but out and out *pornagra*phy.

* * * * *

Redeeming socialness is where they do the same old
pornagraphs but they give ya some four-dollar
words while they're doin' it.

* * * * *

It's Knute Rockne, Edith. And I ain't seen it more than
ten times, so leave me alone.

* * * * *

Because it wasn't one of them nowaday dirty ones
with everyone jumpin' into bed—sometimes three
an' four at a clip! Funny picture . . . I tell you, when
Buster Keaton slammed the spittoon down over that
guy's head, and then took the ballbat and went bin-

go, bángo, bongo! I thought I'd wet my draws.

* * * * *

Archie: Look, I know you'se kids go by what you call this new mortality—skirts up to here—hot pants up to even further—see-through blouses—movies with people in bed—sometimes three, four o' them.

Mike: But, Archie, people's bodies—the fact that they go to bed—they make love it's part of life!

Archie: So's throwing up! But I ain't paying three bucks to see it.

* * * * *

When I wanna learn about pollution, it won't be from no millionaire actor who's got nothin' to do but sit on his duff and dream up causes. If he wants to unpollute something, let him unpollute the movies. All them nudies.

* * * * *

Archie: Well, you shoulda told me that Jane Fonda was in it. I don't wanna go to no movies to hear her mouthin' off about this country.

Mike: When did she say anything about the country? She was playing a prostitute!

Archie: What do you think *that* says about the country!

Edith: When Rita Hayworth played a prostitute, you didn't mind.

* * * * *

ARCHIE ON FASHIONS

I don't want no daughter of mine wearin' nothin' called hot pants. Because hot pants is a derogatory term! When a woman's glands is actin' up and she can't control certain urges—they say she's got hot pants! Same as the meathead there. Hot trousers, hot pants, same thing!

* * * * *

Mike: I love them. To me they're real sexy.
Archie: Well, we can excuse you—you're in permanent heat, anyhow.

* * * * *

Archie: You remind me of Fanny Toohane in them things.
Gloria: Fanny Toohane? Who's she?
Archie: A girl I used to know when we was kids. She'd show you her bloomers for a bite of your jelly apple.

* * * * *

Couldn't you two manage to get a second pair of pajamas? Or would it destroy something beautiful in your marriage? It ain't decent going to bed like that. We go to bed fully dressed.

* * * * *

You wanna help me with somethin' that troubles me? Then put something respectable on. If that thing was up any higher, it'd be a scarf.

* * * * *

Archie: Think of yourself out there in California all year long in nothin' but a blouse and a pair of pants.
Edith: But you don't like me in pants.
Archie: Out there I'll like it.

* * * * *

(*To Gloria*) And pull down that skirt. Everytime you sit down in one of those things, the mystery is over. What the hell *is* it nowadays. Girls wit' dresses up to here, boys wit' *hair* down to here! I stopped in a Gent's Room the other day, there was this character there with a ponytail to here. My heart turned right over —I thought I was in the wrong toilet!

* * * * *

Archie: He's even gonna loan me a coupla them wild, colored shirts that hang out, so's I won't look a tourist.
Gloria: Daddy, I'm surprised you're willing to borrow them. That time you needed one for bowling you wouldn't wear Michael's sweat shirt when

154

he offered it.

Archie: Little girl, there is a big difference between another man's shirt and another man's sweat shirt. Namely, sweat.

* * * * *

ARCHIE ON WOMEN'S LIB

The girls shouldn't count on
Archie Bunker's support.

So that's it, Edith. The cancer's come into our house. I suppose next she'll have you walking around in hot pants and burning your brassieres.

* * * * *

He ain't screwed up enough being a pinko and an atheist. She's gotta make him a half-man, half-woman, too.

* * * * *

All right, Edith, you go right ahead and do your thing . . . But just remember that your *thing* is eggs over easy and crisp bacon.

We *were* into it. Now we're *out* of it. You just tell
your wife to stop putting fancy ideas in her mother's
head. They don't belong there. It's like putting lace
on a bowling ball.

* * * * *

Gloria: Submitting to him. That's what she's doing.
Submitting to her king . . . her ruler . . . her
lord and master.
Archie: Ain't that a nice way of putting it?

* * * * *

A SAGE AND WIT
LOOKS AT THE WORLD

**Down at Kelsey's Tavern he's known as the
thinking man's thinker.**

I don't know what the world's coming to. It's dog eat
dog out there. Some nut decides to throw himself
in front of a subway train and ties it up for thirty
minutes. He couldn't have picked the middle of the
day. He had to pick the rush hour.

*   *   *   *   *

I got nothin' against mankind. It's people I don't trust.

*   *   *   *   *

We got a religious oil burner. It never works on Sunday.

*   *   *   *   *

Just the headlines on the front page could put you away.

*　*　*　*　*

Disney World's gonna be something to see! You know what it cost them to build that Disney World—four hundred million bucks! You got any idea what that comes to in dollars and cents?

*　*　*　*　*

It so happens that Mickey Mouse ain't got no race. He stands for all men. That's why Walt made him a mouse. You know, I was talking to Billy Hartfelder from down at the plant. Now, he's a man of the world—he's been everywhere and done everything, and he's got the tattoos on him to prove it! I mean, he's got tattoos on him he won't even show his wife! So when a guy like Billy tells me that Disney World is the place he wants to go to die . . .

*　*　*　*　*

No, doctors is different. The most beautiful woman in the world walks into a doctor's office and gets undressed it don't mean a thing to him. He don't even notice the good parts. He's thinkin' about where he can stick the needle, where he's gonna cut for the appendix, whether she's gonna pay him in cash . . .

*　*　*　*　*

For twenty-five bucks some of these doctors'll tell ya' anything you wanta hear.

*　*　*　*　*

Insurance companies live to cancel out guys like me.

*　*　*　*　*

Take inflation. Inflation is directly connected to your wage price index which has nothin' to do with the President—'cause *his* wages is fixed by Congress an' so is his price!

* * * * *

I am the breadwinner with three mouths and one giant garbage disposal unit to feed.

* * * * *

Your colored run faster. They jump higher. They don't bruise as easy. And because of their what you call it, jungle heritage, they see a lot better, good for night games. All I'm sayin' is it was unfair to the white ball players . . . who weren't fortunate enough to be born with the same natural endorsements.

* * * * *

There are some nights when I don't think I'm gonna make it through that minefield out there! I go down into the subway—Mayor Lindsay's Toonerville Trolley System—and I ain't never seen it so crowded. I mean it was a wall to wall meltin' pot. Why? The trains ain't runnin' again . . . So I look for someone who speaks my language, and all I can find is this subway guard, one of your pushy Imported Ricans walkin' around inside a uniform ten sizes too big for him. And I ask him real polite—"Hey, Pedro, what's up?" And he says, "The water. It's floodin' over the rails." I says, "How am I gonna get home?" He says, "Try swimmin' up the tracks."

* * * * *

I hadda take a bus—two buses. Dollar five to get home. I tell ya, earnin' a living is costing me money!

* * * * *

If you'll pardon me, you can lump it. Take it down the road and dump it.

* * * * *

How was my day? It was a laff riot, Edith! One jolly moment after another! That's why I'm standin' here—the bluebird of happiness! "Nineteen Robberies Reported in Queens District." Two of them right around here. Yesterday Ryan's Gas Station and this morning, I passed old Lady Krimsky's Bakery—you should have seen what they've done to her—stole 180 bucks, right out of her stocking. Then just for spite busted up the place . . . cheese cakes spattered on the walls—bagels rolling all over the sidewalk . . . We're living in a jungle.

* * * * *

Don't nobody ask me how was my day, you'd not like the answer. Vacate this chair. Edith, how are you? I'm fine. Thank you very much. And that's all the talk I wanna hear outta you until further notice. And a dummy up, meathead to you. And that takes care of this here group. Now hear this, all a yez and pass the word to the kitchen. I got a big problem to figure out. Top level! It's gonna take a lotta thinkin' and it's gonna take all my consecretion. This is where I'm gonna be doin' it. And you're all gonna be helpin' me. How, you may ask? By keepin' your mouth shut. Now synchronize your tongues to silence! Ready? Begin!

* * * * *

No, it ain't a funny name. It's right out of American history. The name's Bunker . . . as in The Battle of . . .

* * * * *

It's a shame Electric Shuffleboard ain't a recognized sport. I could make a real name for myself.

* * * * *

(On the birth of a child
in a stock elevator)

Oh, come on, I don't make myself out no surgeon. I can just handle emergencies, that's all. And I was the only one that had the *Daily News* when it was needed . . .

* * * * *

What about *my* rights? I know I got a lot going against me. I'm white, I'm Protestant, and I'm hard-working—but can't you find one lousy amendment that protects me?

* * * * *

Your good imported cheese is *supposed* to smell bad. The more it smells, the more it costs.

* * * * *

This here's a copy of the Apollo 14 Insignia. That's what separates the U.S. of A. from the Red Chinks and all them other losers.

* * * * *

The Catholic Church owns half of New York! Including some of your finest clothing stores.

* * * * *

This here country was ruined by Franklin Delano Roosevelt! That guy was hangin' on like a Pope.

* * * * *

He wouldn't wear no French watch. He buys American.

* * * * *

Out West, where there's lots of elbow room. Where a man can walk on top of the mountains without people pushin' and shovin', and there you seldom hear no discouragin' words.

* * * * *

(*To a very pregnant young woman*) Believe me, I saw *you*. Meanin' no offense, but you look like one of them jumbo rubber dolls that you punch to the floor and bounce right up again.

* * * * *

What about John Wayne? And before you say anything, just let me warn you that when you're talking about the Duke you're not just talking about an actor, you're talking about the spirit that made America great.

* * * * *

What is more important than the safety of my family? The defense of our home.

* * * * *

There's a special Providence that takes care of drunks and dingbats. It's their loved ones who suffer and go hungry.

* * * * *

My kid had brains enough to be born in a hospital at four o'clock in the morning—while I was home asleep!

* * * * *

(*To Gloria*) Yeah, that's how I used to get you to go to the dentist. I'd give you a chocolate sundae, a jelly apple, and three nickels for yourself. I was the only one smart enough to know how to handle ya without spoilin' ya.

* * * * *

He ain't colored. He's Polish. What's Civil Rights got to do with Polish?

* * * * *

It's moments like this where the only thing that holds a marriage together is the husband bein' big enough to step back and see where his wife is wrong.

THOUGHTS
FROM EDITH....

... that other Bunker who sometimes has the last—and better word.

Poor Archie! Two big problems at once. That's the trouble with trouble—it always comes in twos and threes. Not like happy things. They only come one at a time. Or not at all.

* * * * *

I was just thinking, when I was a young girl I never knew what every young girl was supposed to know. And now I'm gonna be an old lady, I don't know what every old lady is supposed to know!

* * * * *

See, everybody. Aspirins—cold tablets—cough syrups —vitamins—juice—thermometers—Kleenex.   I've set them all up buffet-style. Isn't that handy?

* * * * *

Look, I think I feel a new wrinkle already! It's like when they left Shrangi-la with Ronald Colman in *Lost Horizons*.

* * * * *

Well, I was going over to see Sybil Gooley, but I called the hospital to be sure about the visiting hours and there was a Mr. Smidley with a hernia in her bed . . . I only hope they discharged Mrs. Gooley before they put Mr. Smidley in her bed.

* * * * *

I wonder why the sandman is Japanese. Why wasn't he an Arab? They have so much more sand.

* * * * *

Edith: Yeah. I saw a picture in the *News* of a young boy frying an egg on the sidewalk.
Mike: Yeah. They show a picture like that every year.
Archie: It's probably the same picture.
Edith: And the same egg.

* * * * *

Mike: What's the big deal? Casual acquaintances kiss today.
Edith: Like Merv Griffin and Johnny Carson.
Archie: Merv Griffin and Johnny Carson do not kiss each other, Edith.
Edith: That's right. They're on different channels.

* * * * *

Edith: You never *used* to mind eating in the kitchen when we lived on Union Street.

Archie: Edith, we were livin' in one room! I couldn't eat in the dumbwaiter, could I?

Edith: There, you see? It ain't eatin' in kitchens you mind. It's dumbwaiters!

* * * * *

"Sex and Health?" What do those have to do with each *other*?

* * * * *

(discussing Edith's menopause)

Gloria: There's nothing to worry about. Look it says in this article right here . . . "Nowadays with simple hormone treatment there are no unpleasant manifestations."

Edith: Well, my Aunt Elizabeth went through this and she didn't get manifestations. She got a mustache.

* * * * *

I like filling them cards out and putting down the serial numbers and imagining them going all the way to places like The American Eagle Electronics Company, Fujiama.

* * * * *

Archie: So that's how it started. The meathead kissed her and caught her germs! And then I just've caught it from him!

Edith: You kissed Mike?

* * * * *

175

Archie: Cut your toenails! . . . Cut them, Edith. And I mean right down to the bone. You got a thing you're doin'; during the night with your feet comin' over to my side and your toe nails runnin' up and down my leg. It's like sleeping with a leopard!

Edith: I'm sorry, Archie. I had no idea . . . I usually know what my toes are doing.

*　*　*　*　*

Archie: How about you, Edith? I mean everyone wanted to be something else. What did you want to be? . . . Anything? Besides married, I mean.

Edith: No, I didn't. But my mother did.

Archie: Aw, your mother! What did she want to be, Edith?

Edith: She wanted to be the mother of a tap dancer.

*　*　*　*　*

If I could only remember it, I could time it by playing the "Minute Waltz." Although the last time I played it, it took seven and a half minutes. Mrs. Kurlinger, my piano teacher, said it was a new world's record.

*　*　*　*　*

Vicino: 'Cause I *saw* who hit me. It was a colored guy. A young black bum! He didn't even *smell* Italian.

Edith: That's right . . . they don't use garlic much, do they?

*　*　*　*　*

Edith: Oh, well, y'see . . . this brand was on sale.

Archie: So what? If dirty socks was on sale, would you buy them?

Edith: No, Archie.

Archie: And why not, Edith?

Edith: 'Cause you already got dirty socks.

* * * * *

Coming *down* the stairs isn't so bad. It's all those ups. Like they say—"Whatever comes down, must go up!"

* * * * *

Wendell: How does he do it, Aunt Edith? Tell me now . . . *How does he do it?*

Edith: Do what?

Wendell: He hasn't aged a day. Not a day. Not a single day.

Edith: Oh . . . it must be them new pink bulbs we put in all the lamps.

* * * * *

Claire: Still . . . something tells me I can reach this man.

Edith: If you want to try through his stomach, the kitchen ain't being used now.

* * * * *

Edith: I guess I was sighing 'cause somehow it don't *feel* like Christmas.

Mike: I know what you mean. You mean we're all kow-towing to Madison Avenue and the Almighty Cash Register. You mean Christmas has become a victim of progress and crass commercialism.

Edith: My! Did I mean all that?

* * * * *

177

Edith: No . . . Archie, this is real. Look, it says . . . "Top Composers, like Richard Rodgers and Burt Bacharach will set your poem to music."

Archie: *Like* Richard Rodgers, Edith. That don't mean you're gonna *get* Richard Rodgers.

Edith: All right, so it's Bacharach instead. What do you want for thirty dollars!

* * * * *

(*Archie* in the bathroom)

Edith: You been in there twenty minutes already.

Archie: It's more like *ten* minutes, Edith, and who made *you* the official timekeeper?

Edith: What are you doing in there, anyway?

Archie: I'm changing a tire! . . . All right, all right! What *is* it with you two tonight? What's so important you gotta pull me outta the only room in the house where I can get a little peace and quiet.

Edith: Ain't that nice, Gloria? He makes it sound like a chapel.

* * * * *

Mike: Boy, that Arch! I mean, here it is, his wife's birthday, and he hasn't got one ounce of sentiment about it.

Edith: Oh, sure he has. You just have to know where to look for it, that's all.

Gloria: Where do *you* look for it, Ma?

Edith: Oh—around the house.

* * * * *

McKinsey: How would you describe Mr. Grundy's drink-

178

	ing?
Edith:	Oh, very well!
Archie:	Edith . . .
Edith:	I'd say he's top on the block!
Archie:	Edith, *stifle*! What my wife means is—
Edith:	Last New Year's, Mrs. Grundy held one leg, Archie held the other, and they pushed him home, hand-over-hand, just like a wheel barrel.
McKin-sey:	We'll just say he's a social drinker, then.
Edith:	Yeah. An exceptional one.

*   *   *   *   *

Archie:	Edith, here it is. Clear as you're ever gonna see it. The two generations. There's the modern one. His wife spends three weeks b.a. with a guy, now she's five hours late gettin' home from that guy and he sits there hummin' away, happy as a bird. That's because his generation trusts, Edith. They trust the blacks, the Puerto Ricans, and the Japs, and the Chinks and the Jews and the Indians, and lastly but not leastly, Hungarians! I'll tell you what they trust. Anything that ain't us. I give that boy my advice weeks ago. I warned him about that Hungarian. I told him there was only one place you could put your trust. In Him. But, did he believe me? Oh, no. And you know why? He don't trust me.
Edith:	How can he? You ain't God.

*   *   *   *   *

179

"I AIN'T NO BIGOT"

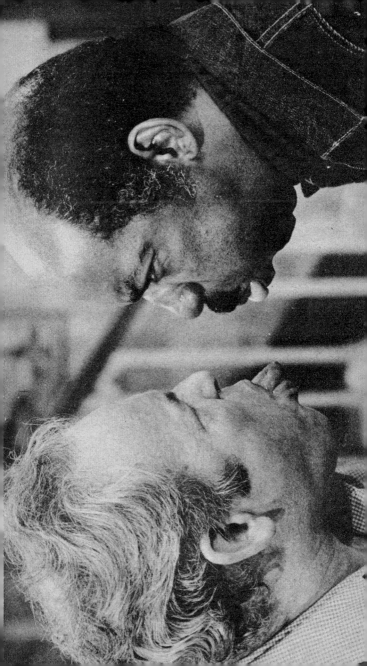

Look, Archie Bunker ain't no bigot! I'm the first to say
—it ain't your fault you're colored.

* * * * *

What's in a name, anyway? They're all a bunch of bed
fumblers. When I was a kid we didn't have no race
trouble—an' you know why? Nobody called themselves Chicanos. Or Mexican-Americans, or Afro-
Americans. *We was all American* . . . Then after
that if a guy was a Spic or a Jig it was *his* business.
I mean it was his business, if he wanted to cling with
his own kind. Which most of them did. That's how
you get your Harlem and your Chinatown and your
Little Italy.

* * * * *

I am not prejudiced. Any man deserves my respect,
he gets it. Irregardless of color.

* * * * *

Archie: He's gonna tell me I'm prejudiced again, Lionel. Can you smell it coming? Do me a favor,
Lionel. Once and for all, tell this meathead
here . . . from your suspective, as one of your

183

regular blacks, tell him where I stand on prejudice.

Lionel: Gloria, Michael. You want to know where *Mr.* Bunker stands on prejudice? He stands firm. Firmer, I think, than anyone I know. And that comes direct from one of your regular blacks.

* * * * *

Listen, you really think I'm prejudiced? Let me tell ya what Sammy Davis, Jr., himself said when he dropped in on the Bunker household that time. Here it is—straight from the horse's mouth:

Sammy
Davis,
Jr.: Now listen, if you were prejudiced you might have thought of me as a coon, or a nigger. But you never said that, instead you came right out clear as a bell and said—colored.

Archie: That's right.

Sammy: And if you were prejudiced you'd shut your eyes to what's going on in this great country, but not you. You can tell black from white, and I have a feeling you'll always be able to tell black from white. And I know if you were prejudiced you'd go around thinking that you're better than anyone else in the world, Archie. But, having spent this wonderful afternoon with you, I can honestly say you've proven to me that you ain't better than anybody.

Archie: Can I shake your hand on that? I hope youse all heard that. Comin' from no lesser man than Mr. Wonderful himself. Now that oughtta prove to youse once and for all that I ain't prejediced.

* * * * *